THE MAKING OF A
ONE-HANDED ECONOMIST

THE MAKING OF A ONE-HANDED ECONOMIST

Gerard Sullivan

Book Guild Publishing
Sussex, England

First published in Great Britain in 2011 by
The Book Guild Ltd
Pavilion View
19 New Road
Brighton, BN1 1UF

Typesetting in Garamond by
YHT Ltd, London

Printed in Great Britain by
CPI Antony Rowe

A catalogue record for this book is available from
The British Library.

ISBN 978 1 84624 570 1

'There's no such thing as a one-handed economist: it's always on the one hand this, on the other hand that'.

Joke quoted in *The Economist* and reported in *The Week*, 28 July 2001

Gerald Ford, the accident-prone President of the United States between Richard Nixon and Jimmy Carter, reputedly once said that he wanted to be advised by a one-handed economist.

To Mary, Sian and Ruth for their love and support always, and especially when I needed it most.

Contents

Acknowledgements

Rather late in the day, I wish to recognise the inspiration I gained from Martin Mwesiga, Frank Mugasha, Yoweri Museveni, Laban Erapu, Shadrach Ekisa and a succession of their fellow sixth-form students at Ntare School, Mbarara, Uganda where I taught in the 1960s. Their stimulating arguments and their friendship were a constant delight and first prompted my interest in the problems of development. I also include in this tribute Joviah Musinguzi, who attended one of my management training programmes in Uganda in 1990 and has kept me regularly informed of events there ever since. My daughter, Sian, cast her critical academic eye over some of the chapters and many of her suggestions have been gratefully incorporated.

Finally, I wish to thank my editor, Jon Ingoldby, for the efficient way he eradicated foibles in the text. Any quirks that remain are attributable to my own fallibilities.

Gerard Sullivan
Chipping Campden, June 2010

List of Abbreviations

ANC	African National Congress
BICC	British Insulated Callender's Cables Ltd
BTRI	Bangladesh Tea Research Institute
BTRP	Bangladesh Tea Rehabilitation Project
CBA	Cost Benefit Analysis
CDC	Commonwealth Development Corporation
CDO	Collateralised Debt Obligation
CDS	Credit Default Swap
CNAA	Council for National Academic Awards
COSATU	Congress of South African Trade Unions
DfID	Department for International Development
DPRD	Decentralised Participatory Rural Development
EDI	Economic Development Institute
EU	European Union
FAO	Food and Agriculture Organisation
HSC	Higher School Certificate
ICA	International Coffee Agreement
ICO	International Coffee Organisation
IMF	International Monetary Fund
IRR	Internal Rate of Return
LDC	Less Developed Country

LDG	Less Developed Garden
MAMC	Mananga Agricultural Management Centre
MDC	More Developed Country
MMR	Maternal Mortality Ratio
NEP	National Economic Planning
NGO	Non-governmental Organisation
NIC	Newly Industrialised Country
NRA	National Resistance Army
NTI	National Training Institution
ODA	Overseas Development Administration
ODM	Ministry of Overseas Development
OPEC	Organisation of the Petroleum Exporting Countries
PDU	Project Development Unit
QE	Quantitative Easing
QM	Quantitative Methods
SADCC	Southern African Development Coordination Conference
SWOT	Strengths, Weaknesses, Opportunities and Threats
TVET	Technical and Vocational Education and Training
UNCTAD	United Nations Conference on Trade and Development
UNDP	United Nations Development Programme
VAT	Value Added Tax
WHO	World Heath Organisation
YEO	Youth Employment Officer

Introduction

I hadn't realised until after quite some time meddling with economics – that's the trouble with being a late developer – that the world is full of one-handed economists. Ambidexterity is out. It used to be thought that impartiality was unequivocally a good thing. 'On the one hand' we used to say, mouthing the viewpoint of some economic sage on an aspect of esoteric theory, 'but on the other hand' voicing the opposite conclusion from some equally renowned economic guru.

This was seen as displaying objectivity – the economist behaving as a scientist. The evidence on both sides had been reviewed disinterestedly and the listening students were invited to exercise their own judgement while the expositor sat on his hands. In this way the economic chastity of the lecturer was carefully preserved. His hands remained unsullied by anything approaching an opinion.

It took years of unlearning to realise that students of the *dismal science* were more interested in what their tutor actually thought than in second-hand distillations from the literature. On reflection, given the aridity of much of the writing on positive economics, this was not so surprising. They recognised their

1

tutor's biases and preferred doctrines anyway, however eloquent his attempts to conceal them with a balanced presentation.

Since students rarely shifted their own ideological viewpoint in deference to this exposure over several months, the revolutionary thought occurred – revolutionary for an academic, which at the time I was – why not advocate certain types of economics? Why pretend allegiance to a dispassionate discipline that appears to be indifferent to pressing economic problems besetting people's lives? Without emotional empathy nothing would change. It took only a further short step to reach the conclusion that so-called mainstream economics was really only advocacy in disguise – particular economic beliefs elevated artificially to the status of a science by the use of scientific-sounding language and an abundance of mathematics. In short, economics was not even-handed but intrinsically one-handed.

This book jogs loosely through my experience of economics in a variety of contexts. It is avowedly anecdotal and should appeal to all those who have an abhorrence of fat textbooks littered with elegant but irrelevant equations. Some might even get a feel for the fun and frustration their studies in economics could lead to if they're not careful.

1

Beginnings

No one who hasn't worked in a laboratory can possibly understand how important this apprenticeship is in the making of the one-handed economist. Latymer Upper School, once a highly regarded direct grant grammar school, in West London's Hammersmith, produced two types of educated male. The fee-paying students spawned by the middle and professional classes who went on more or less automatically to university, particularly Oxbridge, or took articles in law and accountancy, and the 'scholarship boys', sons of the working classes who invariably left school at sixteen, denying themselves the great benefits of a Sixth Form education either through ignorance or inclination.

Emerging from the latter group, my entry into British Insulated Callender's Cables' (BICC) physics laboratory was part of a cleverly devised strategy of career development. A master of my acquaintance at Latymer had received a request from BICC to submit a couple of boys for a research assistant post they were trying to fill. Clearly thrilled that I had passed his

O-level chemistry at the second attempt, he sent them my name and I passed the interview. I had no idea at this stage that I was destined to follow in the footsteps of Richard Feynman – which was just as well since I wasn't.

Not to put too fine a point on it, my formal relationship with physics lasted precisely four months but provided a quality learning experience. Although unrecognised at the time, it was my first exposure to 'The Scientific Method'. This is a procedure by which trainee research assistants do all the empirical donkey work while the graduate scientists write the papers, get the credit and are more highly paid. It was an early lesson in the division of labour. Specialisation distances you from the rest. The farther away you are from the real work the greater the rewards.

The specialisation in this case was brown paper, crucially important at that time for insulating cables. The varieties were enormous and consignments of samples from around the world kept arriving at the laboratory for testing. It is difficult to wax eloquent on the properties of brown paper, which most people would probably agree is not a particularly sexy subject for scientific exploration. They would be right – its dullness is outstanding and survived everything we did to it. This is not quite true. The dullness was not so much inherent in the brown paper but in the behaviour we exhibited towards it.

Even at sixteen I had this vague notion that research was glamorous – it was about making new discoveries and pushing back the frontiers of knowledge. Somehow this perception never penetrated the experience of a morning crouched over a micrometer taking one thousand thickness readings to three decimal places of a small piece of brown paper. Neither did it enter my head when wedging successive tiny fragments of the stuff between two silver papered electrodes under oil and measuring its capacity to withstand an incremental electric charge until the current eventually burst through.

We weighed it, stretched it, measured it, heated it and electrocuted it endless times and yet its significance eluded me. Analogies with wood and trees spring to mind. It was all unutterably boring, relieved only by the prospect of Fridays spent at the local technical college skiving through A-level courses one was never destined to complete and numerous games of table tennis after work with fellow sufferers in the works canteen.

Perhaps it was the trappings of scientific endeavour that I couldn't stomach. The electrical tests, for instance, were conducted, if you will excuse the pun, in a prison-like building full of caged equipment. The cage was penetrated by arms with metal balls on the end which were manually brought together to complete an electrical circuit. The repetitive nature of the test numbed the senses. Maybe the sentenced research assistant hastened his parole by increasing the current too quickly or was guilty of bringing his balls together too violently, thus distorting the readings. Who knows? The subsequent results, as with most statistical representations of reality, acquired a concreteness of their own belying any misdemeanours in their collection.

It was a sobering thought. Here I was, dabbling with one of the hardest of 'hard sciences', admittedly on its lower slopes, only to find that it had a soft, or at any rate malleable, centre. Its conclusions rested on shifting sand echoing Heisenberg's famous 'Principle of Uncertainty'. Yet later, I was to learn that this was the ultimate goal sought by certain positive economists anxious to earn status by turning their subject into a real science like physics or chemistry and to rid it of offending adjectives like 'political' or 'social' associated with its historical origins.

But we run ahead of ourselves. As a consequence of this short sojourn with physicists, somewhere lurking in my loft is an esoteric research paper written by a graduate scientist on the insulation properties of brown paper with second billing given to one G. Sullivan. As Michael Caine would say, 'not many people know that'.

It is tempting to say that I left BICC behind but it is more honest to say that they left me behind. BICC went on to become a giant international corporation ending up as Balfour Beatty. I entered the City.

This was another carefully orchestrated career move and one which first taught me the iron law of planning: 'be in the right place at the right time'. The right place at that time was the Youth Employment Officer's room in Carmelite Street. After an hour scratching his head tortuously trying to decipher the inner workings of the sixteen-year-old's mind, the telephone rang. It was the Chief Clerk of the Guaranty Trust Company of New York searching for recruits. The YEO put down the telephone and said, 'How about banking?'.

Within a week I was translated from white-coated apprentice physicist to dark-suited city gent. The

6

bridge between C.P. Snow's two cultures had been crossed – well almost. It may not have been the arts and humanities but it was certainly a million miles away from the environment of science. For a start there were girls. Clearly, banking had advantages over science and I began a two-year love affair with the City.

It was ten years after the Second World War and the Guaranty occupied some rather elderly buildings in Lombard Street – number thirty-two to be precise – which in turn were occupied by some rather elderly clerks commuting daily from south coast resorts ready for retirement. An influx of teenagers like myself began to change the rather staid atmosphere. We revived the football team, ran in the inter-bank cross country races and patronised Humphrey Lyttleton's traditional jazz concerts at the Conway Hall.

New entrants to the bank usually did a stint on the journal, juggling the day's credits and debits in a space behind the cashiers' box where we could see top-hatted bill brokers trading their bills in units of £500,000. A spot balance with my colleague of both sides of the journal at £31 million on one occasion was something of a record. After three months in this lowly position we were dispersed to other departments. My fate was 'Securities'.

Transferring stocks and shares on behalf of the bank's clients opened the mysteries of the Stock Exchange, introduced its actors, the brokers and jobbers, and its menagerie of animals, the bulls, bears and stags. 'A bull buys expecting a rise; a bear sells fearing a fall' or words to that effect. In those days there was something to look down on from the public gallery as the brokers registered transactions with the jobbers setting out their wares against the pillars on the floor of the Exchange and 'blue button' messengers relayed information on prices back to their stockbroking firms. Trying to make sense of this ant-like, scurrying activity struck the young observer with a sense of awe. It was magical and strangely romantic. This was the heart of the City, the centre of things and you were a small part of the action.

Just how small became clear when the bank wanted you to run errands. I often wonder how many economists physically handle treasury bills? I did, on several occasions, walking around to the side door office at the Bank of England to exchange maturing three-month bills for new ones peeled off the Bank official's pad. On another occasion I had a 'spear carrier's' role in helping to reduce the money supply. A Gladstone bag of gold sovereigns was chained to my waist and carried by the bank's six-foot messenger escort, while I held his truncheon, around to the vaults of Robert Benson Lonsdale, merchant bankers, for shipment to America. A taxi was required for this escapade and I dread to think what might have happened if there had been a hold-up and thieves had made off with the bag in another vehicle. 'Unidentified flying bank clerk spotted in the City' might have been the headline in the evening papers.

It was during my time at the bank that I had my first sighting of an economist at the City of London College, Moorgate, where young bank clerks were encouraged to attend evening classes in preparation for the Institute of Bankers examinations. It was not a good role model and for years afterwards my image of the archetypal economist was coloured by this experience. It seemed to be *de rigueur* to be dishevelled in dress and a smoker with an infinite capacity for loquacious prattling. He was off one night and his enthusiastic young replacement thrilled us with his demonstration of Keynes's insight into the equality between savings and investment. Then it was back to the smoking tramp.

The Institute of Bankers itself was at the other end of Lombard Street. Its lounge (or was it a library?) was sumptuously furnished with large armchairs affording ample space for post-prandial snoozes by older members on rainy lunchtimes. Occasionally, invited speakers gave talks. These rarely disturbed the sleepers. One of them was given by the legendary Professor F.W. Paish; legendary because of his advocacy, in the halcyon days of 1 per cent unemployment in the 1950s, of running the economy with 3 per cent unemployment. Then, as now, distinguished professors were not noted for the alacrity with which they applied such theorising to themselves by rushing off to join the dole queue.

On this occasion he was going on about 'consols'. Since neither my colleague nor I knew at that stage that this was the shortened version of 'consolidated stocks', much of his talk sailed above our heads. What I still remember is that for weeks afterwards we chattered on endlessly back at the office about the state of consols without a clue what they meant. It became one of our standard jokes, like saluting with black-rolled umbrellas, the insignia of all City staff, as we parted for the tube each night.

Here I wish to drop a name. For some of the bank's

football matches I travelled pillion on a friend's Lambretta motor scooter. He was a few years ahead of me, a high-flier in the bank and destined for greater things. Just how great became clear when I saw his picture in *The Economist* offering his opinion on the world monetary situation. He was (Sir) Dennis Weatherstone, who became President of J.P. Morgan in 1987 and then group chairman and chief executive from 1990 to 1994. His obituary appeared in the press in June 2008[1].

It was in Moorgate that I discovered the law of diminishing marginal utility and another lesson for the budding economist: get some jargon under your belt. Apart from its relevance or otherwise it comes in handy when you want to amaze friends at cocktail parties with your erudition. The more obscure the jargon, the more esoteric it sounds and the greater your prestige.

Very roughly the so-called law of diminishing marginal utility refers to the common-sense observation, 'the more you have of a thing the less satisfaction you get out of it'. More precisely, it claims that after a certain point is reached in the consumption of units of a good, say, apples, the extra satisfaction derived from consuming one more unit (i.e. marginal utility), not surprisingly, begins to fall. It will continue to diminish as more units are consumed. The question is, at what point does a person stop consuming apples? This is where the sleight of hand comes in. Most ordinary people would say that the body has ways of indicating when it has had too much of a good thing,

---

[1] See *The Daily Telegraph*, 28 June 2008.

which we need not go into here. The economist would claim that consumption of a good would stop when the price of the last apple eaten exactly equals the satisfaction (utility) it yields to the consumer. The trouble is, this doesn't quite explain how a quantitative measure, price, can ever reflect a qualitative attribute, namely, satisfaction.

Nevertheless, later in life, this slight technical difficulty never stopped me and no doubt many others from regaling endless groups of students with fictitious scenarios proving the validity of this law. My favourite always involved making a member of the group a cross-country runner (always good for a laugh) who arrived back at the clubhouse after a ten-mile run gasping for a drink and proceeded to slake their thirst by drinking pints of beer. They were willing to pay much more than its price for the first pint because they were so thirsty but successive pints were valued less highly and so on until the pint equating price and marginal utility was reached.

There are other technical problems that limit the law's application. For instance, not all goods are divisible conveniently into small marginal units. If a person collects vintage cars, who's to say that the last one purchased gives less satisfaction to the owner than previous acquisitions? I suppose if someone goes to the theatre thirty times to see the same play, it could be argued that their satisfaction was diminished by subsequent visits after the first performance, but who would be crazy enough to do such a thing?

The *piece de resistance* is the attempt to apply the law of diminishing marginal utility to money so that, as before, the more you have of it the less satisfaction you gain from it. By this logic, shedding some monetary wealth will leave you better off in terms of satisfaction! Until recently one didn't see much empirical evidence of rich people rushing to obey this version of the law. Even now, analyses of charitable donations suggest that wealthier people are proportionately more parsimonious in their giving than those on lower incomes. But there are notable exceptions, like billionaires Bill Gates and Warren Buffett, who are starting a new fashion for spending large chunks of their wealth on foundations supporting good causes.

All this talk of satisfaction may have led me to question the utility of spending my youth rearranging the investments of rich American clients. At any rate, armed with my Institute of Bankers Part I examination I left the City to serve Her Majesty for two years' national service in the Royal Navy. As far as I know, Her Majesty was not aware of this.

During my five days at sea – the rest of the time was shore-based, spent on what were affectionately known as 'stone frigates' – I had my first brush with the Mafia. I had managed to get away from Chatham Barracks to Malta for the last five months of my service by volunteering to take a friend's draft. He had just got married and with typical naval precision they immediately planned to post him abroad. I volunteered a second time to get on board the submarine depot ship, HMS *Forth*, which was permanently based at Malta but had an annual foray into the Mediterranean to see if it could still float. It could, and two days later we landed in Sicily.

Three uniformed matelots sauntered into Palermo to sample its delights on a drizzling afternoon. On thirty-five shillings a week I couldn't manage much sampling but my friends were 'regulars' (i.e. long-service ratings) and therefore comparatively rich, which was just as well as things turned out. We made for a café. Very soon we were engaged in conversation with a friendly local who just happened to have a friend who had a car and might be willing to show us the sights outside Palermo. He was, and arrived with another friend. The six of us piled into the car and shot off to see an old mountain-top hotel used by the Gestapo during the war, a church sunk into the rock eerily hung with celluloid parts of the body that its members wanted the reclining gold saint to heal, as well as some of the surrounding countryside.

After some conversation between our guides on the way back to Palermo from this whirlwind, but fascinating, tour, the car inexplicably stopped. Friendly man number one explained that his friend the driver wanted payment for this joy ride. We had naïvely thought it was an exercise in Anglo-Sicilian relations. The fare asked was, of course, extortionate. We carefully weighed up our negotiating strength in a sheepish exchange of looks, wedged as we were on the back seat of a two-door Volkswagen Beetle behind three Mafia types presumably armed to the teeth with stilettos, and meekly paid the ransom. The British Navy did not exactly cover itself with glory in this incident but at least I learned, unwittingly perhaps, the importance of producer power in forcing consumer demand.

Flown out to Malta towards the end of national

service the expectation was that HMS *Phoenicia*'s pay office, which housed most of the writers keeping the accounts for the ships in the Mediterranean fleet, must be deluged with work. In fact it only occupied half my time and I managed to persuade the Education Officer to take me on for the other half. He didn't need much persuading as with an assistant to open up the library and small education office he had more time to sleep off his daily hangover from the previous night's jollifications in the wardroom. Nonetheless it offered the splendid perk of access to all the new books and magazines arriving for the library and an after-office-hours quiet venue for studying an A-level. Part of my duty also involved coaching other ratings with one-to-one tutorials in elementary mathematics and English, which stood me in good stead for my next foreign venture some six years later.

2

Uganda Beckons

'Hold the line, please.'

The secretary's voice faded away and I was left musing to myself about the outcome as I waited for her return. Looking back on it now, I suppose it was one of those moments of suspended animation when the summer limbo of 1964 would suddenly end and the future, or at any rate the next two years of it, would equally suddenly be decided.

The voice belonged to what was then called the Department of Technical Co-operation. It subsequently became known as the Ministry of Overseas Development, abbreviated with typical Civil Service subtlety to the initials 'ODM' so as not to be confused with the Ministry of Defence. Later it was transformed into the Overseas Development Administration (ODA) and is currently called the Department for International Development (DfID). Its status has also been advanced since it is now headed by a Secretary of State who sits in the Cabinet, rather than a mere minister who did not. Despite the constant re-branding, one of its continuing functions is to act as a clearing house between overseas governments requesting technical assistance, which in the early post-independence period took the form of armies of teachers, agriculturalists, engineers and other so-called 'experts' to help with their development programmes, and people in Britain who for one reason or another have a yen to work abroad.

Yards of correspondence over the years with this post-colonial institution enquiring about overseas opportunities, which must have tried the patience of even the most resourceful filing clerk, has left me somewhat uncertain as to whether this bureaucratic bridge-builder actually facilitates or frustrates the endeavours of these two groups to come together. Be that as it may, in the summer of 1964, somewhere in the ODM labyrinth lurked an application form with my name on it. It had languished there apparently undisturbed for several months since my interview. The reason for the telephone call was to discover whether it was still flowing down ODM's mainstream decision-making channels or had been steered into some backwater for terminal cases.

The enquiry was not without some urgency. I had recently finished a three-year teachers' course at Dudley Training College and a further year at Regent Street Polytechnic to complete a London University BSc (Economics) degree and was poised to launch myself on an unsuspecting school public. For some obscure reason, since I had never been gripped by that irrepressible vocational urge to teach that infects some members of the profession but saw it as a means to travel, I was being encouraged to bid for a post at an enlightened comprehensive school in South London.

An innovative married couple in charge of economics and commerce at Malory School had visited Dudley to talk to students and afterwards noted my name as a possible additional member of staff when I graduated. In due course, I spent a day at the school and was most impressed by the relaxed atmosphere and the quality of the work. Now the time had arrived to enter the job market, contact was renewed with the husband and wife team who informed me that miraculously a new post was being advertised. A form subsequently arrived unsolicited on a Friday which if I was interested was to be returned before the selection committee held interviews on the following Monday evening. Leaving aside the jargon-ridden fact that I appeared to be cast as a monopsonist in a rigged market, by any standards it would make an excellent starting point for a raw recruit into the teaching profession: a school run by a head teacher with vision, in a happy atmosphere, with no discipline problems and progressive colleagues. If I ignored the persuasive overtures coming from South London, what would happen if my efforts to teach abroad came to nought? Hence my dilemma and the hurried telephone call to the ODM.

'Hello, Mr Sullivan.'

The telephone had crackled into life again as telephones do.

'I've found your notes. You've been transferred from the "Teachers for East Africa Programme" to the "Uganda Government Scheme". We'll be sending details of your appointment and a contract shortly.' With that the disembodied voice clicked off the line, unaware of the significance of its simple message and the repercussions that would flow from it.

17

The dilemma had been resolved. I would be going abroad after all and in the ensuing months there would be little time to reflect on the mysterious process by which one arrives at such life-changing decisions. Of course, it would be too much to argue that one chance telephone call had changed everything. *On the other hand* – I was still in the unreconstructed stage – without it, there was at least the possibility that the delights of London in the 'Swinging Sixties' might have postponed my desire to travel indefinitely. Who knows?

In due course the contract documents arrived. The words 'Education Officer' leapt from the pages. The title gave me a sneaking satisfaction. Having failed to convince the Royal Navy's Selection Board that I was officer material back in 1957, I had been awarded a commission at last! The appointment was with the Uganda government to teach economics for a 21– 27 month tour of duty. It was to be located at ... Ntare School, Mbarara. An atlas was quickly consulted and revealed that Mbarara was a small town about 170 miles south-west of the capital, Kampala, towards the border with Rwanda. So that's where I was heading for the next two years.

Once the country in which one would be working was settled, a strange alchemy contrived to make it spring into consciousness at every turn. After being virtually oblivious one moment of the pearl of Africa's existence, a kind of heightened perception then took over, picking out Uganda connections in all directions. The newspapers, for instance, seemed to feature articles on Uganda every other day. A young friend's schoolmaster had taught there recently. The service foreman of a local garage had worked in Uganda before independence, and so it went on. Each of these sources provided another snippet of information which was fastened on eagerly in an effort to expand the narrow image of Uganda that had been acquired incidentally. Just how limited was the picture is rather embarrassing to recall at this stage, a memory only partly eased by the fact that most acquaintances who learnt of the impending trip abroad were under the illusion that Uganda was part of South Africa – a sober reflection on the parochial British perhaps, or a critical comment on our education. At any rate, my image of East Africa merely comprised recollections of distant geography lessons with maps of Y-shaped rift valleys, coloured slides of smiling African children at church missionary meetings and wild animal films at the cinema set in steaming jungles full of chattering monkeys witnessing torrid love scenes frequently interrupted by marauding lions. Not a lot to go on but hopefully the next few years would do something to diminish such incredible ignorance. Getting there was the first problem and a number of hurdles, largely domestic in character, had yet to be overcome.

For anyone unused to travelling out to live in the tropics, a vanishing breed judging by the number of young people flocking along the statutory passage to India and the Far East from the 1960s onwards in search of mysticism and meditation, the actual mechanics of setting off were rather daunting. To begin with there was a deluge of forms to fill – passport applications, next-of-kin statements, Official Secrets Act assurances and the contract itself. Next the luggage arrangements had to be organised and decisions made as to what should be sent air freight for immediate requirements on arrival and what could be managed without until a later date and consigned with a prayer by sea. Rumour had it that British Council officers reckoned they hadn't won their spurs until their sea luggage had gone astray at least once in their careers. The business of packing and dispatching luggage was for this writer the most tiresome and tiring aspect of moving abroad, leaving a backlog of exhaustion to overcome when one actually stepped onto the aeroplane. For later trips the lesson had been well learned and the professionals were invited in to take care of other shipments.

Numerous injections then had to be secured to afford protection against endemic tropical diseases. This was not something I relished since I had never quite got over the shock of queuing up as a naval recruit between two sick-berth attendants who proceeded to puncture one arm with a needleful of smallpox vaccine at the same time as the other arm was being stabbed with anti-tetanus toxoid. It was a traumatic experience and an acutely humiliating one for me as I managed to faint in the middle of their performance. Fortunately, there was only one bad one this time, TAB, which left me low for about thirty-six hours as it did most people. I now know that even that discomfort can be avoided. The secret is to have the injection done intra-dermally, into the skin, but it requires a skilful nurse who's passed her test with the needle.

Amidst all this hive of activity in the run-up to departure, which had been fixed for 6 January 1965, there was a welcome interlude. The ODM in its wisdom recommended all appointees about to undertake their first overseas assignment to go on a week's residential briefing course at Farnham Castle. It is difficult to imagine a more pleasant setting in which to be briefed. It may seem incongruous at first to be meeting in that most English of settings, a medieval castle and one not long vacated by the Bishops of Winchester, to discuss with other travellers the likely hazards to be encountered when living and working in a developing country, but nevertheless it seemed to work. Talks were given by visiting speakers well familiar with the countries to which the thirty or so members of the group were going and embraced the history, political structure and general socio-economic development of the region concerned, in this case East and Central Africa. Other sessions dealt with domestic matters, health safeguards, finance and taxation, and baggage arrangements. There was also an opportunity for private study in a resources room which had available letters and tapes from expatriates currently working abroad and a well-stocked library.

Representatives from the various countries covered on the course and people home on leave provided up-to-the-minute details at informal gatherings in the evenings. A highlight of the course I attended was when Sir Walter Coutts, the erstwhile last Governor of Uganda[2] ended his talk by flashing his Uganda tie out of his waistcoat and saying, 'These are Uganda's

---

[2] After independence the incoming government of President Obote agreed to the appointment of Sir Walter Coutts as Governor-General of Uganda.

21

national colours and this is its national anthem.' At which point he broke into song and rendered the complete version with throaty gusto, much to the amusement of his audience.

It has to be admitted that there was in the 1960s a faint colonial flavour about Farnham, enhanced by the private club drinking arrangements, with everyone on the course automatically a temporary member and settling their bills at the end of the week. An enclave atmosphere was bound to be created given that the group had a common prospect in view and was closeted in a castle for a week to explore its various possibilities. Then again, many of the staff and visiting speakers had done a stint as colonial civil servants before independence or as expatriate officers after it. There was also a strong missionary undercurrent with morning prayers a feature of the daily programme for those who wished to attend. In short, Farnham captured the main influences which had pervaded the colonial period in British history and characterised the translation of a tight empire into a loose Commonwealth.

Inevitably, during the course one was encouraged to examine one's own likely role in the aftermath of such significant social upheavals and in countries continuing to undergo rapid development and change. The value of Farnham lay in orienting one's thinking towards the country in which one had decided to work and it therefore marked the first step in relaxing the ties with home. The next step would be taken with somewhat more confidence in the light of the knowledge gleaned from the course. Before that time arrived, however, there was for me one other matter to be resolved.

Teacher training colleges had a renowned reputation as marriage bureaux. Not only did they offer professional training, they frequently forged professional partnerships as well – as a kind of fringe benefit. This duality of role not altogether surprisingly affected me and many of my contemporaries at Dudley. In consequence, it raised the question of whether I should take a wife to Uganda. Almost without knowing it, another leap-in-the-dark issue was demanding resolution prompted by official travel forms needing to know one way or the other.

This, too, was fraught with complications. It is an understatement to say that Mary's parents were not exactly enamoured of the idea of marriage in the circumstances. Her father, a shoe shopkeeper in the Black Country, believed that Wolverhampton and, more especially, Molineux, home of the famed Wolverhampton Wanderers football team, was the capital of England if not the centre of the universe. The prospect of seeing his only daughter disappear into the bowels of Africa for a couple of years did not hold out much appeal. As an equally entrenched Londoner seduced by the outward-looking mores of that cosmopolitan city, I found such insularity virtually incomprehensible. Add a touch of the Tory versus radical argument to the relationship and confrontation was almost guaranteed. Every argument was used to try and dissuade us or, at any rate, Mary, from making such a move. Better to wait and get married after I had returned was the theme.

Paradoxically, a man who had been a staunch Methodist all his life, a Church which put itinerant ministry at the centre of its missionary endeavour, could not bear to see his daughter depart on a secular journey to Africa. Apart from anything else, escaping from the shop on a Saturday before Christmas was asking too much of any natural born entrepreneur. After all, it was the height of the slipper season!

Eventually, 2 January 1965 was the date settled for the wedding. Fortunately, Wolves were playing away that day. The details of that social event need not detain us. Suffice it to say that the day itself was one of wintry perfection, crisp and sunny. The bride looked beautiful, ate everything in sight and thoroughly enjoyed herself. The groom had stomach-ache, ate nothing and in his speech stoically muttered a few feeble jokes about how wonderful the bridesmaids looked in father-in-law's shoes and warned guests visiting the couple in their new home to watch out for elephants in the garden, before driving away from the reception in neutral. Ludlow and The Feathers afforded a glorious two-day honeymoon respite. Then it was back to Wolverhampton for family farewells and on to London for more of the same. On 6 January 1965 we left for Gatwick to catch the VC-10 for Entebbe and our two-year honeymoon in Uganda.

3

Expatriate Economist

I can still recall the excitement as a boy of seeing bananas for the first time in London after the Second World War. In an entirely different context, one of the earliest Uganda images recorded on Mary's ancient 8mm movie camera is of a man sitting on a mountain of bananas on the back of a lorry as we drove from Entebbe airport to Kampala. There was something odd about them though: they were large and dark green. Later I learned that there are over a hundred different species of banana and that these were called *matoke*. Peeled, boiled and then mashed like potatoes they were the staple food for the majority of the population. These plantains were predominantly grown in a wide swathe around Kampala in the Kingdom of Buganda. Their husbandry was easy in the fecund dark-red earth around the capital so that a lazy farmer could watch them grow from the relaxed confines of a beer garden if he chose. According to one view, such banana-watchers held back the country's development by preventing diversification into other crops and enterprises by trapping huge tracts of land in a near monoculture. Another raises the issue of whether to grow 'cash' crops earning foreign exchange from exports or 'food' crops for subsistence. These were to be recurring themes in my teaching, but let's get to Mbarara and unpack first.

A couple of days were spent in Kampala registering our arrival officially, for which purpose we were booked in at The Grand Hotel with its bathroom towels still initialled 'Imperial Hotel' as a reminder of how recently Macmillan's 'wind of change' had blown Uganda towards independence in 1962. It was here I made my first cultural *faux pas*. Coming down for dinner on the first evening, the Ugandan head waiter marched us through the entire length of the dining room to a table adjacent to the kitchen door. Many other empty tables were passed *en route* so I asked him why we couldn't sit at one of them to which he replied that I was not wearing a tie! Uganda straddles the equator and the temperature hovers around 75–80 degrees Fahrenheit most of the time, but jackets and ties had to be worn in Kampala's premier hotel. Clearly, the British colonialists had left their mark.

The second mistake was not cultural but mechanical. We bought a car to drive to Mbarara. Perhaps it was our limited budget or the fact that our trawl of the garages along Kampala Road came upon one with a former British army major as sales manager who quite by chance had a son at the same school as Mary's brothers, but we plumped for a Vauxhall Viva. It must have been the only one in East Africa. Fine as a second car around town and on tarmac but it couldn't cope for long on the corrugated murram dirt roads traversing most of East Africa. Several breakdowns later, after about eighteen months we traded it in for a Peugeot 404. By then we had realised that there were only three cars that did well on dirt: the bottom of the range VW Beetle, the middle of the range Peugeot and the plutocrat-class Mercedes. Strangely, given that the country was a former British Protectorate and hence a captive market, apart from the ubiquitous Land Rover, there was no British competitor to the 'big three'.

Leaving Kampala behind, we managed to Viva our way to Mbarara and discovered Ntare Senior Secondary School nestling on a low hillside about a mile out of town. It was a boarding school and the students were drawn from all over the country apart from some Sudanese refugees from the conflict in southern Sudan and Rwandan refugees – Tutsis escaping the earlier massacre by the Hutus in the late 1950s.

Entrance to the school was on the basis of primary school examination results. It transpired that Ntare vied with King's College, Budo, near Kampala, for the mantle of best academic school in the country. This meant that at the annual meeting of secondary school headmasters to allocate primary leavers to their new schools, Ntare could cream off those with the best results. The Sixth Form students were among the most talented in Uganda and my task was to teach them economics and British government as part of their Cambridge overseas Higher School Certificate (HSC). If the latter sounds somewhat ludicrous, my historian colleague in the next classroom was teaching the Tudors and Stuarts, even more anachronistic! Yet the boys thrived on it. They were the most dedicated, hard-working students I could wish for in my first proper teaching job, hungry for knowledge, ready to ask questions and willing to discuss issues arising from the work.

Of course, the motivation was obvious. A good HSC from Ntare was the passport to one of the three constituent colleges of the then University of East Africa and a degree from Makerere University College in Kampala, or its sister institutions in Nairobi and Dar-es-Salaam, the gateway into high status appointments in government and the professions. There were often hidden pressures from home too, especially if they were the first generation to reach secondary school from their family or village and fees had been difficult to raise. Some had waited a long time to get this far in the education system and were in their twenties and in one or two cases I suspect older than their teacher's twenty-seven years.

In its wisdom, Cambridge University offered scope among the usual diet of micro- and macroeconomics which comprised the standard A-level type package, to develop some applied economics relevant to the countries in which it was taught. The HSC examination paper had a regional section to test students' local economic knowledge. Imagine the chagrin of Ntare's Sixth Formers one year when the examination paper contained questions asking them to demonstrate the workings of the economies of Sabah and Sarawak! If we'd got their regional questions, perhaps they'd got ours, producing equally puzzled faces on the other side of the globe. Despite such occasional hazards it was amazing to think that in numerous countries around the world, on a particular date, hundreds of students would be writing papers emanating from the brains of a group of academics in Cambridge. The mind boggles.

'Right, gentlemen. Today's topic is "the location of industry".'

I then proceeded to wax eloquent on why Britain had a car industry as a result of specialising in the resources it had available in abundance such as iron ore and limestone to produce steel and a highly skilled labour force plus the presence of power and large markets from dense populations in Europe. On the other hand (Whoops!), East Africa lacked these resources and focused on the production of agricultural products and their processing for which it had abundant natural resources. All straightforward stuff in the textbooks of the day which I merrily spouted forth until I was stopped by a raised hand. A tall, serious looking student had a question. 'Why shouldn't East Africa develop its own car industry?' he asked.

I repeated what I had already said, thinking he hadn't understood. He remained unconvinced. He understood all right, but disagreed with the reasoning. After all, Britain had been primarily an agricultural country until well into the nineteenth century. Why, in principle, couldn't East Africa follow suit? Japan, too, had very few natural resources other than fish, but was a world leader in car manufacturing and electronics. I had been trotting out standard bourgeois economics which favoured advanced industrial economies. Yoweri Museveni, for that was the student, had asked a fundamental question which stopped me in my tracks. As I write, Museveni has now been President of Uganda since 1986.

In a sense we were both right. The mainstream economic analysis I outlined reflected the culmination of a long secular process and as such was essentially static and ahistorical. What Museveni was hinting at in his question was a development strategy that Uganda could work towards achieving – in a nutshell, industrialisation. This exchange with Museveni was an early sighting of one-handedness in economics: advocacy of a belief in a particular economic policy. His own writing, typified by the following quotation, reflects a flowering of the same argument.

> When it comes to the detailed examination of the industrialisation process, we have to find the means of interlinking the different sectors of the economy. You cannot have industries unless you have raw materials for them. These raw materials come from agriculture, from forests, from minerals and, in the case of Uganda, from fresh water resources. Therefore, you cannot meaningfully talk of integrated industrialisation without modernising these sectors of the economy.[3]

He then goes on to expand his theme of modernising agriculture by introducing specialisation and exchange so that subsistence peasant farmers over time transform themselves into rural businesses by concentrating on a few crops sold in markets for money which, when spent, fuels other enterprises. Here it's perhaps worth noting that the 'cash' crops

---

[3] Museveni, Y.K. (1997) *Sowing the Mustard Seed: The Struggle for Freedom and Democracy in Uganda.* London: Macmillan.

versus 'food' crops issue referred to earlier is really a false dichotomy since surpluses of food crops can also be cash crops when sold in local markets.

I wonder if Museveni had in mind Mr Mbide when he wrote his book. Milk and matoke were delivered to Ntare School by Mbide who drove his clapped-out lorry every day along dirt roads from his farm about twenty miles outside Mbarara, deep in the Ankole countryside. Apart from providing education, schools help to develop their local economies by creating demand for other services, and suppliers like Mbide spring up to meet those needs.

It is a false assumption to think that all subsistence farmers have the flare to become farming entrepreneurs. They don't. Most of them are trapped by what Michael Lipton calls the 'survival algorithm' where innovation might risk the harvest of the staple crop which feeds their families. Ugandans are luckier in this respect since the land and the climate conspire to produce lush vegetation over much of the country. For this reason, at the height of the troubles during Amin's reign of terror, when inflation was rampant and basic foods scarce in towns, one of my former students, Frank Mugasha, remarked that in a subsistence economy like Uganda people rarely starve. Even urban workers would still have kinship links with the rural areas and would retreat there if necessary.

Mbide, then, was something of an exception and to learn his story I took a group of students, as part of their economics education, on a visit to his farm. There was a strong element of luck in the saga of his success. He had been befriended by an English

31

colonial civil servant who had made him a gift of £200 before leaving the country. With this windfall he set about developing his land and cattle. For the latter he built cattle dips to protect them against tick-borne disease and had them regularly examined by the veterinary officers. He added to his landholdings and as well as extensive matoke banana plantations had planted coffee over a wide area. As already noted he supplied not only Ntare but other schools and institutions around Mbarara and built up a reputation for reliability and good quality produce selling to these markets. A big, congenial man, he worked hard maintaining high standards of husbandry on the farm and personally driving the lorry distributing his goods off it. He dressed simply in sandals and shorts and lived quite modestly, too. Although his house would have been considered relatively large it was no better than the school's staff bungalows and was not lavishly furnished.

At the end of the farm tour he invited us all to a drink of Coca-Cola and entertained us to a rendition of 'God Save the Queen' of all things, accompanied with his concertina. The boys were suitably impressed and I was, too. Here was a man who by dint of hard work and a bit of luck had literally turned himself into a rich, successful, agricultural businessman. A development model perhaps? Certainly overseas aid officials visiting Uganda often beat a path to his farm to see what they could glean for their policy prescriptions.

To escape classroom learning on another occasion we organised a much more ambitious industrial visits trip to Kampala and Jinja lasting a few days. My own exposure to such visits as a student teacher in Dudley, organised by an enlightened head of department, convinced me that actually being inside a company or looking around a factory and raising questions afterwards with management went a long way to flesh out the textbook descriptions of industry. It also provided senior students with an opportunity to test the waters for possible careers.

Jinja was the main industrial area of Uganda, located near the Owen Falls Dam on the Nile where it left Lake Victoria and the source of hydro-electric power. Here we visited the copper smelting plant converting the ore transported by rail from the copper mine in the foothills of the Ruwenzori Mountains on the border with the Congo, and the Nytil textiles mill fed by raw cotton grown in the northern region of the country. We also took in the Indian businessman Madhvani's large complex of industries based on sugar as well as another textile plant some distance out of Jinja.

At Nytil we saw a brand new workshop stuffed with new machines imported from Britain and managers who supervised operations straight from the declining textile industry of Lancashire. Whilst older machinery was clattering away elsewhere producing fabrics we learned that, with the new investment, Nytil would have the capacity to satisfy the whole of the East African market. Yet there was another textile factory down the road at Madhvani's, a third in Kenya and a fourth in Tanzania. It doesn't take an economic genius to work out that there was excess capacity for the region as a whole and each plant would find it difficult to run profitably. Rationally, and two-handed economists are nothing if not rational, it would seem sensible to reach agreement between the three countries where to locate large industrial investments to avoid such unnecessary duplication. This was at a time when the relic of the colonial East African Community, which ran railways, airlines, postal and other services across the three countries which also formed a common market, offered a vehicle for such negotiations and planned development to occur.

Unfortunately, it was also a time when newly independent states needed to flex their muscles and operate autonomously, which eventually saw the dismemberment of the regional institutions as each state went its own way. More specifically, Uganda and Tanzania sought to escape from the dominance of Kenya and Nairobi as a magnet for capital investment from abroad. Interestingly enough, Museveni sees the East African common market being resurrected as local manufacturers recognise the benefits of a larger integrated regional market.

Prior to the trip a deputation from the students requested that we include a courtesy call on the President while in Kampala. The thought had not occurred to me as it was a bit like dropping in on the Queen at Buckingham Palace on an educational visit to London. In Uganda, it was not at all far-fetched and it was duly arranged that we should see President Obote at the Parliament buildings in Kampala. Leaving aside subsequent analysis of Obote's first administration in the minefield which comprises Uganda's post-colonial politics, it struck me at the time that here was a man who understood the need to respond to the enquiries of the rising generation of intellectuals, many of whom would soon be making their careers in government. For more than three hours he answered their questions ranging over the whole field of government policy and economic development. Critics among them from earlier political discussions back at school were certainly more understanding of the government's problems on their return to Ntare as our post-mortem on the trip revealed.

Jumping ahead for a moment, one of the edifices erected by the time we left Uganda in 1969 bore the President's middle name. It was the Apollo Hotel, for his full name was Milton Apollo Obote. In classical mythology Apollo was the son of Zeus and, appropriately for a politician, sometimes called Loxias: 'the Ambiguous'. The hotel was a tall, slender building which was commandeered by Amin and his army bully boys during the 1970s, falling into disuse and disrepair some years later. After Museveni eventually won power in 1986 and began the process of recovery and reconstruction, the Apollo was transformed into the Sheraton: an even bigger and more splendid hotel rising like a phoenix from the ashes. There is a macabre footnote to this episode. When the developers moved onto the site having cut through the jungle surrounding the dilapidated Apollo, they entered the building, opened the lift and found a skeleton standing inside clutching a briefcase.

4

Market Mysteries

African markets are fascinating and the one in Mbarara was no exception. Sellers displayed their wares on a mat on the ground in front of them where they sat. Fruit and vegetables were carefully built into small pyramids of varying sizes but with the same price and there were many people selling the same goods. While some people looked after the 'stalls' others were cooking food in the background. There was much banter and laughter going on and the place was full of colour, both from the produce and the clothes worn by the traders. It was a social scene and entertaining for the minority of expatriates wandering around in the crowd deciding with whom to do business.

The fun and games began when we stopped by our selected pyramid of passion fruit, say, and after a greeting, *'Oraire gye?'* (Have you passed the night well? i.e. good morning) asked, 'How much?' as the prices were not displayed. It was rather different to shopping at Marks & Spencer. At the reply we would automatically be convulsed with laughter and, with arms waving, dramatically start to move away while uttering negatives at the outrageously high price being charged but, in reality, waiting to be recalled. The call duly came and this haggling ritual continued in a friendly fashion until a bargain was struck.

The question is, was it an equilibrium price?

Now, I was a fresh young economics graduate who was supposed to know something about demand and supply, so had I accidently stumbled on the holy grail of the textbooks' perfect market? Certainly there were a number of buyers and sellers, the products were fairly homogeneous and the market area was small enough to get around all the vendors, so shoppers had perfect information even if the final deals were struck at different levels. Given the buying power of the expatriates, you always knew when it had been abused and the trader beaten down to a rock bottom price as the smile was wiped off their face.

Be that as it may, buyers and sellers of a good were definitely in contact with each other which defines the existence of a market, but did it clear at the bargained price? I don't know, but I suspect that at the end of the day some vendors had unsold produce, the fresh stuff would be going off and prices would have eased to avoid having to trek home with it. Mbarara market seems a simple enough thing. People grow crops on their small plots of land, some for their own needs and the rest to try and sell in town for money. Markets for exchanging goods and conducting trade have existed for centuries and, according to Karl Polanyi, trade was always regulated in some way, either by tribal practices and social customs or by national statutes under mercantilism.

What complicates matters and elevates this ordinary human activity into a philosophical ideology is the claim from some quarters that the whole economy should be governed by markets. As Polanyi puts it:

> A market economy is an economic system controlled, regulated and directed by markets alone; order in the production and distribution of goods is entrusted to this self-regulating mechanism.[4]

This is a relatively modern idea. Elaborate explanations of how the market performs this trick appear in every standard textbook on economics. In essence it's all done by signals. Consumers signal their demand for a good by buying it. If they want more of it than producers have put on the market the latter can raise its price. If they were already covering their costs and making a profit, they are now making an even bigger profit. Price signals will start lighting up further down the production line, attracting other owners of resources and land, and workers with the right skills, to move into this expanding area of production, persuaded by the prospect of earning interest on their capital, higher rents and better wages.

There's more. Where the characteristics found in Mbarara market are widespread throughout the economy and competitive conditions prevail, only the most efficient, lowest-cost producers will survive. Cunningly, consumers rule the roost by not only deciding what is produced by their expenditure

---

[4] Polanyi, K. (1944) *The Great Transformation: The Political and Economic Origins of Our Time*. Boston, MA: Beacon Press.

patterns – or demand – but also by getting their goods at the lowest prices. Make no mistake, this beneficial outcome comes about, paradoxically, when everyone is acting selfishly in their own interest. Consumers naturally want to buy at the lowest prices to maximise the satisfaction they can get from spending their incomes, and producers naturally want to sell at the highest prices to maximise the difference between their sales revenue and their costs of providing equipment, land, buildings and labour to produce the goods – which is their profit. Despite their selfishness in doing what comes naturally, consumers and producers reconcile their conflicting interests in a multiplicity of markets in which everyone is a winner. This represents the enduring appeal of the ideal of a freely functioning market economy under conditions of perfect competition. The beauty of it all for the proponents of this market mirage is that the whole signalling network runs by itself without any interference from government.

Unfortunately, any number of examples can puncture this glossy picture. Let's take one from Uganda with which I'm familiar, namely, coffee. In the 1960s, coffee was the second most important commodity, by value, entering international trade after oil. It was, and still is, Uganda's most valuable export. It is grown by hundreds of small farmers on their two- or three-hectare farms along with other crops for household subsistence. At that time, coffee was experiencing one of its periodic gluts on the world market, the effect of which was to depress the price. What should our rational coffee producer do?

According to the market model, faced with an

excess supply situation he should reallocate his resources into some other form of production and get out of coffee. In fact, the reaction in Uganda was often to plant more coffee to try and sell more at the lower price in order to maintain income at a certain level. It takes about four or five years before a new tree yields a crop and if large numbers of growers behaved in the same way, future gluts might be even worse. Alternatively, new plantings may have taken place in response to an earlier shortage on the world market which caused a rise in the world price. The lagged response of the increase in production has itself created the depressed price. Nothing can be predicted with certainty, however, in the coffee world. There is always the possibility of frost, real or imagined, in Brazil (the dominant producer and exporter) severely denting its output and strengthening the world price of coffee.

'Coffee is virtually synonymous with crisis' I wrote with a flourish in 1972 at the start of an article in *Barclays Review*,[5] not simply to try my hand at hyperbole. It was a prelude to the forthcoming negotiations for the renewal of the International Coffee Agreement (ICA) in which a crisis was certainly looming. Without going into the labyrinthine technicalities of the actual operations of a global commodity agreement – worth a PhD in itself – suffice it to say that it was like the Mbarara scene writ large but with traders bargaining on the world stage. It was a power play. In one corner was the United States, devouring nearly half the world's production and other western

---

[5] *Barclays Review*, August 1972: 'Coffee – grounded?'

countries supping the rest. In the other corner was Brazil with roughly one third of the world's coffee quota under the Agreement and the rest of the world's producers mainly in other parts of South America and Africa.

There were two other key ingredients in the situation. Firstly, coffee is produced by less developed tropical countries and is consumed mainly in richer industrialised countries, which emphasises the traditional conflict of interest between low-price seeking consumers and high-price seeking producers. Secondly, the persistent crisis associated with coffee stemmed from an endemic excess supply situation. On the demand side, consumption of coffee rises only slowly. We don't suddenly move from drinking three cups a day to ten. In contrast, supply can be dramatically increased as, for example, when Brazil opened up the state of Parana to coffee production following the price boom in 1954. Hence the international Agreement was designed, in theory, to regulate the amount of coffee entering world trade by awarding countries an export quota. When there's a glut depressing prices below an agreed floor, quotas are adjusted downwards. Conversely, when prices rise above an agreed ceiling, quotas are revised upwards. Juggling the quotas is meant to stabilise the market and, in this case, the coffee price.

It sounds reasonable enough but the trouble is producers resisted calls for increased quotas when prices were booming because that's what they really wanted, not stable prices. Likewise, American roasters in particular opposed reductions in quotas when prices were falling through the floor. Given that some countries were not members of the Agreement, the whole regulatory machinery was difficult to manage since outsiders could to some extent undermine it. Even the members didn't always keep their word. Eventually, any attempt to regulate coffee prices was abandoned and in the most recent agreement of 2007 the objectives are largely about the collection and sharing of information on production and consumption of coffee by member countries and providing a co-operative forum for the promotion and strengthening of the global coffee market.

Violent swings in commodity prices – 'the slings and arrows of outrageous fortune' – can be devastating to a developing country like Uganda, heavily reliant on one or two export crops to spearhead its development. Foreign exchange earnings finance essential imports for transforming the economy by boosting its industrial sector. Fluctuations in the value of coffee exports have serious repercussions on Uganda's investment programmes and long-term growth.

I learned some years ago from the Ugandans running their Coffee Marketing Board's office in the City of London that not even Amin at the height of his malicious reign dared to interfere with their work. He knew only too well that the flow of earnings from coffee exports lubricated the anarchical horrors of his army's thugs.

Given the vulnerability of an economy such as Uganda's to the vicissitudes of trade in a single commodity (and it's even worse for the archetypal 'banana republics' of some of the Caribbean islands), is it any wonder that they would like to bend the market in their direction? The so-called 'free' market has done them few favours and some would argue that Adam Smith's celebrated 'invisible hand', which leads an individual who 'intends only his own gain ... to promote an end which was no part of his intention' (i.e. society's interest), has developed arthritis. Smith is usually quoted out of context. He was attacking excessive regulation of international commerce under the straightjacket system of mercantilism. He advocated that entrepreneurs should focus on employing their capital in domestic industry for profit, not that their goods should monopolise the home market to the exclusion of foreign products if the latter could be made more cheaply. As such, he was perhaps the first one-handed economist.

Freedom from over-regulation, however, does not necessarily mean no rules whatsoever. If the freed-up system benefits some players to the detriment of others whose very economic survival is threatened, what should the victims do? There was a time in the wake of the Organisation of the Petroleum Exporting Countries (OPEC) oil price hike of 1973 – which for that commodity dramatically shifted power away from oil importing countries and in favour of oil exporting countries, many of which were in the developing word – when copycat moves for other internationally traded products became a distinct possibility.

What were the essential features of a successful producer's cartel which could shift the price upwards? The commodity needed to be pretty indispensable without close substitutes which would be consumed instead if its price rose. Secondly, it required a 'Saudi Arabia lookalike' dominant exporter that could control the supply stocks and oblige other producing countries to comply with the agreed policy. Thirdly, the latter point meant success was more likely if the bulk of the export trade was concentrated in the hands of a few countries. Fourthly, an efficiently supervised system for monitoring production and trade flows had to be instituted. Finally, a high degree of trust between members of the trading club was essential to make the market intervention work.

OPEC had these key features in spades for quite a long while and contrived to engineer the price of oil upwards from $3 a barrel in 1971, to $11 a barrel in 1974 and $43 a barrel on the Rotterdam market by 1980. As a result, OPEC's current balance of payments moved from a surplus of $2 billion in 1972 to a surplus of $120 billion in 1980. In the face of these figures, there is no denying the power commodity producers can wield if they collaborate. The question is, could other producers get their act together and 'do an OPEC'?

I thought at one time that it might just be possible for copper and coffee to follow suit as they had quite a few of the necessary conditions outlined above. The United Nations Conference on Trade and Development (UNCTAD), with an acronym translated by some wag into the wonderfully apt mnemonic – 'Under No Circumstances Take A Decision' – was much more ambitious and, in the mid-1970s, promulgated the idea of international agreements for seventeen commodities. This was accompanied by a panoply of initiatives to create a 'Common Fund' which would finance buffer stocks, encourage cartels, promote diversification away from dependence on one or two export commodities and fund research. This surge towards a New International Economic Order was led by UNCTAD's members from less developed countries (LDCs) and challenged by members among the more developed countries (MDCs). One or two agreements were launched but the grand schema gradually drifted into the sand. Clearly, it was an idea whose time had not yet come.

Meanwhile, back in Uganda, Tom Ellis was putting forward ideas at the micro level for dealing with low-priced coffee. Tom Ellis, an ex-Indian army major with Indian Mutiny silver on the dining table to prove it, was Principal Assistant Agricultural Officer for the Western Region of Uganda. As such, he was responsible for promoting coffee in the districts of Ankole, Kigezi and Toro.

We have to bear in mind here that the first ICA was established in 1962 and export quotas were introduced for 1963/4. Curiously, the International Coffee Organisation (ICO) for administering the ICA was located in London's West End in 1963, in a country that doesn't produce a single coffee bean.

Major Ellis's strategy had a straightforward objective which was for Uganda to earn a growing amount of foreign exchange from its key coffee crop. He was talking to my Sixth Formers, many of whose fathers were coffee growers. It was 1967 and already Uganda's allocated quota had been substantially cut by nearly a third from its original level of circa 150,000 tons in 1964 against the background of excess supply and falling world prices. He had a two-pronged approach. Prong number one was to increase the unit value of the crop produced. Prong number two was to cut back over-production. Coffee is not a homogeneous good but comprises two basic types, arabica and robusta. At the time, arabica commanded a huge price premium over robusta. To increase the value of the crop, since it was total export which was limited by quota, the aim was to get farmers to switch from growing robusta to arabica. Farmers were assisted financially to uproot robusta coffee trees and replace them with other crops. Along with these policies, Major Ellis focused on improvements in quality at every stage of processing, with his eye on the achievements of Kenya in developing a distinctive brand image worldwide for high quality coffee.

At no time did Major Ellis suggest sitting back and just leaving it to the market. The world of coffee, as with other major commodities entering international trade, away from the heady atmosphere of alliances and conflicts fought out in negotiations at the ICO, affects thousands of people around the world struggling to make a living growing it on their smallholdings. They need a voice to represent their interests, bend the market in their favour and protect them from its worst consequences. The measured words of Professor Amartya Sen, the first Indian Master of Trinity College, Cambridge University, can serve to round off this excursion: 'the market mechanism is an essentially incomplete specification of a social arrangement'.

5

CBA And All That Jazz

At this point in my personal economic odyssey, I suppose it's fair to say that I shot my first ideological rapids. The unadulterated frictionless market is a myth. The economy does not progress via a series of smoothly adjusting markets towards some heavenly equilibrium, nor does it ever achieve an optimum use of scarce resources. This nirvana is only perceived in the elegantly constructed mathematical models purporting to describe such a state of economic bliss. It doesn't exist. It's like Monty Python's 'dead parrot'. It is deceased. It is no more. We leave it behind on one side of the river near the far bank – a metaphorical oxbow lake isolated and cut off from the main flow. We emerge downstream on the other side and step into the blindingly rational light of the new ideological paradise of planning. Phew! I enjoyed that.

Amazingly, nearly all the administrations of the newly independent former African colonies prepared a five-year development plan a few months after taking office. Amazing because if Britain is anything to go by, the former colonial powers themselves, with the possible exception of France, never indulged in such exercises. So why did development planning become so popular?

Maybe expatriate advisers thought that now was their chance to experiment with economic planning. Certainly, there was a view held at the time, perhaps unkindly, of Scandinavian economists working in Tanzania that the country's economy was so bad that none of their interventions could possibly make it any worse. No doubt also, British experience of consumer rationing, regulated trade, centralised production and currency controls, successful during the war, still conditioned the thinking of some latter-day development administrators. That experience, as A.J.P. Taylor put it, 'produced a revolution in British economic life, until in the end direction and control turned Great Britain into a country more fully socialist than anything achieved by the conscious planners of Soviet Russia'.[6]

On the ideological front, the idea of a 'command economy', comprehensively planned and led by the state, was rigorously being implemented in the Soviet Union from the Russian Revolution of 1917 onwards. At one level it appeared to be working, too, since within fifty years it had dramatically transformed a peasant agricultural economy into a leading industrial power so that it ranked almost on a par with the United States. Leaders of other peasant economies were bound to take note.

To whom was this great transformation attributed?

---

[6] Taylor, A.J.P. (1965) *English History 1914–1945*. Oxford: Oxford University Press, p. 507.

Who was the intellectual colossus whose ideas underpinned this revolution, the bearded rationalist who conceived this planned Elysium? Enter, stage left of course, that arch villain, Karl Marx. Cast in a villainous role by critics who feared his revolutionary fervour in mid-nineteenth century Britain, one suspects that the real reason for the continuous onslaught and condemnation his name has wrought is because he touched a raw nerve. His insight into the nature of capitalism exposed aspects of the behaviour of capitalists they would rather have kept hidden. Far from being the best thing since sliced bread, for Marx, the capitalist market economy did not automatically reconcile the conflicting interests of individual consumers and producers in a host of decentralised markets for products and services. That gloss belongs to the later doctrine of neo-classical economics described earlier which emphasised consumer sovereignty, scarcity of resources and their optimal allocation. Instead, Marx argued, capitalism produced chaos in the form of irrational market fluctuations throwing people out of work into an 'industrial reserve army'. This pool of unemployment kept the wages of workers at the subsistence level necessary to reproduce their labour power and a ready source of supply of replacements for anyone who dropped out of the active labour force.

Granted, the analysis was drawn from Victorian society experiencing the hardships of growing urbanisation enforced by industrialisation, but it had powerful echoes for anyone trying to understand the violent slump in production and trade leading to massive unemployment in the Great Depression of the 1930s. It also had resonance for Third World countries (as they were then referred to) in the second half of the twentieth century, mainly engaged in subsistence agriculture with only an embryonic industrial sector and where large numbers of people were thought to be unemployed or underemployed in rural areas.

Hence planning became the watchword for nationalist governments anxious for faster economic development now that they had thrown off the yoke of colonialism holding them back. That Marx was awarded the authorship of this approach is curious in the light of his own words: 'Society is a sort of organism on the growth of which conscious efforts can exercise little effect'.[7]

In reality, five-year plans mostly consisted of wish lists of development projects which governments sought to undertake with outside help from international aid agencies. Each of these projects would be subjected to a cost benefit analysis (CBA) estimating the rate of return on the resources invested. The pot of funds available would be drawn down according to a pecking order of projects derived from their estimated contributions to the economy.

CBA is conceptually straightforward. For an agricultural project, for example, the net returns to farming of the existing system are calculated by subtracting current costs of production from the gross value of production. Call this estimate, A. The net returns to farming of the proposed scheme under the

---

[7] See John Macdonell, 'Karl Marx and German Socialism', *Fortnightly Review*, 1 March 1875, vol. xvii, p. 391.

project are similarly calculated. Call this estimate, B. Subtracting A from B will estimate the net receipts from farming due to the project. These benefits are then compared with the construction and maintenance costs of the project to see if it's worthwhile going ahead. If the benefits outweigh the costs then 'bingo', we're in business. Unfortunately, the devil is in the detail as we shall see later.

George Sacker was responsible for my first brush with project appraisal. He was manager of Uganda's Ankole Ranching Scheme (ARS), a project designed to turn fairly empty grazing land outside Mbarara into a hundred roughly equal ranches. A system for allocating the ranches was devised which, since one of the main criteria was ownership of a certain minimum head of cattle, meant that the scheme inevitably benefited the relatively wealthy cattle owners. Aspects of the project included establishing valley water storage tanks, cattle dips, a breeding station staffed by several vets to experiment with crossbreeding local Ankole cows with exotic animals in an effort to increase meat and milk yields, and a pasture improvement programme in the hands of a single pasture agronomist – my great buddy, Graham Harrington.

Apart from his PhD in grass, Graham was one of life's originals, a proactive person if ever I saw one. A monthly amusement for some of the expatriates was a play-reading group with copies borrowed from the British Council in Kampala. Not content with this, Graham got us to put on a play, Ann Jellicoe's *The Knack* which, after performances in Mbarara, we then staged at the National Theatre in Kampala. Not only that, he managed to persuade my wife, who had never acted before, to take the only female part. In its day *The Knack* was quite an *avant-garde* and amusing probe into power games and sex with three likely lads trying to make it with a girl from the provinces who happened by looking for the YWCA. One had the knack, one wanted to acquire it and the third was a kind of referee. The sight of Mary in one scene perched on top of a stepladder scantily clad in babydoll pyjamas yelling, 'Rape, rape, rape!' at the top of her voice in front of an audience of bemused Ntare schoolboys left an indelible mark on my memory.

Graham also managed to drag me up the splendid Ruwenzori Mountains on the border between Uganda and The Congo on two of my four expeditions, and wrote the most creative entries in the Bijuku Hut log book. One wonders what subsequent climbers made of his description of the first ascent of Mount Speke by the latrine variation. Maybe it's the altitude but men on mountains seem to be somewhat pre-occupied with their state of health and basic functions which give rise to what might seem to others low anal humour. My weekly wartime diet as a boy, of Andrews liver salts, Scott's emulsion and syrup of figs meant that I was an easy target for some of these jokes. On one occasion, after an hour baring my soul on the lower slopes of the Elena Glacier and returning triumphantly to the hut like the ghost of Titus Oats, I was awarded 'bonus points' by the rest of the party for scoring on the ice. This became the gold standard for the rest of the trip and was followed by much speculation as to what scientists several hundred years in the future tracking my spoor would make of these rock-like droppings.

After that necessary diversion let us return to the ARS. In 1968, George Sacker organised an international conference in Mbarara on beef cattle breeding and ranching, attended by academic researchers and development managers and planners from around the world including a high-powered delegation from Botswana headed by the Vice President. Not long before the conference, George, who I did not know very well, came to see me slightly alarmed that nothing in the highly scientific papers he and his colleagues had prepared for the conference attempted to provide an assessment of the likely economic impact of the project. He felt that his financial flank might be exposed – not a pretty sight as he was a large man – if he couldn't demonstrate, when asked, that the considerable investment of resources and technical personnel into his sizeable project was making a substantial contribution to the economy. As the nearest thing to an economist outside Kampala, could I help?

I accepted the challenge with more alacrity than I had competence to manage at that stage and immediately felt my first attack of one-handedness coming on. The point was not to ask what good this project was doing for Uganda but to provide evidence that it was beneficial. The conclusion was contained in the premise, namely:

All projects are good.
The ARS is a project.
Therefore the ARS is good. The bottom line, so to speak!

55

It seemed that all I needed to do was find a method of estimating the monetary value of the project's net benefits. A veil was drawn over the possibility that the investment costs might conceivably outweigh the expected benefit stream from new incomes. Surely not. I scurried to my thin library of economics texts and discovered the long since discredited notion of 'secondary benefits'. If the initial valuation of increased production and incomes directly derived from the ranches as a result of the project fell short of the costs, what about adding those indirectly boosted by the project like the extra incomes for local butchers and dairymen, transport firms distributing the products, road gangs maintaining the service roads and the retail outlets in Mbarara and the nearby villages?

The magic word 'multiplier' now comes into play, suggesting that the initial investment expenditure gives rise to a ripple effect generating a dying wave of additional incomes and expenditures. What's more, this great Keynesian insight can be quantified so long as we know the value of another lovely piece of jargon: the 'marginal propensity to consume'. This simply means the proportion of new income people spend on consumer goods and services. Suppose they spend three quarters of their extra incomes then a bit of elementary mathematics can show that the value of the multiplier is four.[8] Hence the total increase in incomes is four times the original injection of investment.

The first round of expenditure becomes direct

---

[8] Formula for calculating a simple multiplier: $m = 1/(1-mpc) = 4$.

income to the suppliers of labour and resources to the ranching scheme. Subsequent rounds occur when the recipients spend a proportion of their new incomes. These are all secondary effects to the primary purpose of the project which is to increase the value of meat and milk outputs in the project area and hence the incomes of those involved in their production. Clearly, the multiplier coefficient depends upon the assumed value of the marginal propensity to consume which is at best a guess without systematic surveys to estimate it more accurately. It is, however, but a small step to make sure that the assumed value is sufficiently generous to indicate – surprise! surprise! – that the total benefits of the project outweigh its costs.

I shudder to think now of the hazardous figures along these lines that I calculated and which were subsequently published after some massaging by George Sacker, in the *Proceedings of the Conference* which validated the worthwhileness of the project. Perhaps it did not really matter in the long run because, sadly, I have to report that a contact in Uganda informed me through the wonders of email at the start of the new millennium that the ARS did not survive intact. Land and animals were confiscated without compensation and redistributed to other cattle keepers, dams have never been de-silted and other infrastructure has been run down.

At the time, however, I was elated at having a first taste of development planning. My appetite grew after hearing the government's Chief Economist, a British expatriate, explaining the thinking behind Uganda's Second Five Year Plan in a lecture given in Mbarara.

One thing struck me in particular. The plan made no provision for around 60,000 of the children leaving primary schools to have secondary education. I taxed the speaker on this. What were they going to do? He looked blank and muttered something about seeking employment in the informal sector of the economy, a euphemism for hawking or petty theft. Alternatively, they would have to be absorbed in agriculture back on their parents' plots of land. In my naïvety I was aghast to learn that there were no plans to expand the secondary sector to enable children to continue their education. It dramatically confirmed the privileged status of Ntare School's students and the extent to which they had striven to be creamed off and arrive at the apex of the educational structure.

Was this just the stark reality of economic life in an LDC with not enough resources or were they being badly managed? I needed to learn more about this planning lark. It vexed me that there were no proposals for remedying the situation over time and that thousands of children would have to abandon their formal educational development halfway through. With this in mind, I decided to leave Uganda in 1969 at the end of a second two-year tour and return to school to study how to become a development economist. This transpired to be a wise move before Idi Amin came to power in 1971, wreaking havoc and abruptly ending those, for some of us, halcyon days. Needless to say, his *coup d'état* while President Obote was attending the Commonwealth Conference in Singapore was welcomed by the British government irritated by Obote's declared policy of 'moving to the left' which they saw as heralding greater interference

58

with the business activities of British companies, especially the banks.

I had secured a place at Birmingham University to do a postgraduate diploma in national economic planning which seemed to have the right ring about it. While I had been languishing in the post-colonial sunshine, the discipline of economics had been colonised by mathematicians. This meant that the leisurely journey home by sea was punctuated by frequent sessions in the lounge of the *Windsor Castle* trying to penetrate the intricacies of differential calculus and matrix algebra so that I was up to speed and could hold my own by the time I had to meet the young Turks on the course who no doubt had devoured such techniques with their mother's milk. In fact there were no Turks, young or otherwise, but five Iraqis, a Japanese, a Sri Lankan, an Indian, a Pakistani, a Kenyan, an Irishman and two Brits.

Into this cauldron of nationalities was poured a mixture of enthusiastic young academics making their mark launching the new National Economic Planning (NEP) unit and a couple of mad professors. Of the latter, Dr H. was Dutch and spoke haltingly in English. Given the international complexion of the course, many of the students were also not entirely fluent in English. His subject was econometrics, a complex new mathematical economic language most of us had some difficulty in grasping. It was a double linguistic whammy. Dr H.'s lectures, delivered on the move so that his constant pacing threatened to wear a groove in the floor, came across in a high-pitched, strangled voice in a tongue barely recognisable as English, and dealt with esoteric concepts at a level several dimensions above the comprehension of his audience. It was the fastest-shrinking class in academic history. Faced in a week or so with only two bewildered Iraqis who were probably writing letters home, the group was declared inquorate and Dr H. resumed what he liked best: churning out undecipherable and probably unread books and journal articles.

Professor K. was equally eccentric. His specialism was conflict theory and he proceeded to analyse the possibilities of a third world war and the standoff between the super powers with the penetrating insight offered by a two by two matrix. He was a simple man. Fortunately, the up and coming young academics knew their stuff, worked us hard and we became quite proficient in the operations research techniques underpinning the planning of resources, to the extent that I was able to apply a linear programming model to Uganda's agricultural diversification problem for my final special study which had made no sense at all at the start of the course. All the same it felt a bit like taking a sledgehammer to crack a nut. Then again, it is one thing to discover from the available data which crops and in what quantities at the macro level farmers ought to be growing to maximise returns. Making it happen was something else. From my experience of Uganda, I knew it required a quantum leap to change the economic structure and implement my carefully calculated solution. Although invited to stay on for another year, I therefore opted to continue my studies elsewhere even though it was quite a wrench leaving my 'United Nations' friends. Armed to the teeth with algorithms and clutching my Birmingham Chamber of Commerce prize, I switched to Leeds University to take a masters degree focusing on the financial aspects of economic development.

A little over two years after leaving Uganda, bristling with two more credentials, I was ready to return in a new capacity, that of economic planner. Unfortunately, the market had dried up.

6

Wadi Wanderings

In spite of the assurance by the man from the ODA, after he had addressed our group at Leeds University, that there would be lots of openings for a newly qualified chap like me who already had overseas experience, there was nothing. It seemed that the emerging administrative cadres graduated and doctored in economics before most other subjects and they naturally filled the posts in their own countries. Visions of square pegs and round holes started to haunt me. After a few months when the postman's daily visitation deposited 'regret' slips through the letter box, I decided to act. The unfettered market was not removing my personal unemployment problem. It needed some help. After all, I had a wife and daughter to keep and another baby on the way, a situation calling for drastic action.

I marched on London, my home town. Back in Lombard Street, I requested a meeting with the Personnel Manager of Barclays Bank's head office and scored a bull's eye with my first dart. They just happened to need another economist in the Economic

Intelligence Department. Intervention had worked where *laissez-faire* and planning had both failed. I had discovered The Third Way a few decades ahead of Anthony Giddens. However, before turning again like Dick Whittington towards London, another opportunity came my way by a circuitous route.

Back in Yorkshire it transpired that a Bradford University professor and a Leeds University senior lecturer working as economic consultants to Sir William Halcrow and Partners needed to replace a third member of their team. The assignment was to conduct an economic appraisal of the United Nations Food and Agriculture Organisation's (FAO) Wadi Jizan Irrigation Project in Saudi Arabia. This was just the sort of thing I was looking for and I persuaded Barclays to put my appointment on hold to enable me to undertake it.

My task was to work on the data so far collected from the project area and then carry out a month's fieldwork to plug any gaps and in particular to repeat a livestock survey. The first one had been conducted by my predecessor gathering farmers in one centre and getting their responses to questions by a show of hands. For some reason this was regarded as rather unscientific and meant that the data produced was even more suspect than that I more systematically collected later with an administered questionnaire.

Wadi Jizan is in southern Saudi Arabia on the border of Yemen. The project area was about thirty miles inland from Jizan Port on the Red Sea where the office was located. Halcrow's assignment was to design an irrigation scheme to improve agricultural production from crops and livestock in the area in the wake of a dam having previously been built which provided a measure of control over the flash floods periodically descending from the mountainous interior down the wadi. With an annual rainfall of only two to four inches, the need to maximise the utilisation of water was crucial.

The credibility gap between the academic and practical approaches to CBA quickly became apparent. I also soon discovered the different emphasis given by agriculturalists to the problems of development compared with engineers. Halcrow employed a small army of the latter and as lead consultants engaged other agencies to contribute supplementary specialisms in, for example, aerial surveys, land tenure, agricultural and economic analysis. The agriculturalists tended to adopt an evolutionary stance, building on existing farming practices and improving them gradually over time, working with the grain of rural institutions. The engineers seemed to have a penchant for spreading concrete around the place at least until the early cost figures suggested that it was not economically viable. Then they were quick to innovate alternatives. To that extent they were inclined to be more radical.

Meetings at Halcrow's head office in London's Notting Hill Gate resolving the tensions between these professional interest groups were a revelation. Much of the heated discussion was about what crops should be grown once the new irrigation scheme was in place and whether cotton should be introduced as a new cash crop. This would impact on how much land was devoted to the traditional grain crop, dura. The Guyanan Project Engineer, Bob Comacho, was very keen on cotton and had vast experience of other projects in the Middle East where it had been successfully established. The agriculturalists were much more sceptical and produced figures in support of their view from schemes showing declining cotton yields after an initial burst of high performing years. Then there were arguments about irrigation structures, how many diversion weirs there should be channelling water from the dam's controlled releases along the wadi onto farmers' land and whether they should be made of concrete or utilise existing earth 'barrages'.

It has to be admitted that in sorting out some of these issues the finer points of academic CBA methodology tended to be glossed over by project practitioners. Theoretically, CBA is a decision-making tool for choosing, in the Wadi Jizan context, between alternative irrigation possibilities and cropping patterns in the project area. In practice, early in the life of the appraisal project, Bob Comacho, wearing his other hat as Principal Water Engineer, walked the length of the wadi and on the basis of his experience decided the number and position of the proposed diversion weirs, seven in total. Halcrow's field staff, supplemented from time to time by visiting specialists, proceeded to collect the data to flesh out this project design.

It was not until some months into this work that it dawned on someone, hopefully the economists but I have a memory lapse at this point, that the CBA technique is meant to enable a choice to be made between competing uses for the resources. Five other variants were then magically conjured up within

Halcrow's head office offering alternatives using lined and unlined distribution canals below only one main diversion weir and different sizes of canal. The differing water flows these schemes generated in turn meant different estimates for the hectarage of irrigated land and hence the amount of production. The final report could then present neat calculations for the internal rates of return (IRR) for the six projects. The ironic *coup de grâce* was to recommend the original version of the project, on which most of the investigatory time and effort had been spent, even though its IRR was not the highest. The choice was justified with some nifty rhetorical footwork about not burdening Saudi administrators with future construction work from conceivably faster siltation rates from some of the other schemes with better rates of return.

This is common practice among consultancy firms continuously engaged on project analysis and validating their recommendations in accordance with the requirements of international funding agencies. It does, however, beg the question of why undertake the elaborate pretence of employing CBA to improve decision-making when the actual decision to proceed or not with a project is taken on other criteria.

Admittedly, the procedure does have the virtue of getting those involved with the design of projects to think carefully about the implications of their proposals. But is that enough when the valuation of one key variable, with some judicial tampering, can be sufficient to lift a project's rate of return above an arbitrarily chosen rate for viability, usually around 8 per cent, and give it the green light? London's Victoria

Line got the go-ahead in this way when commuters' travel time savings were reassessed.

Perhaps even worse, an expensive economic appraisal can be commissioned to allow an informed choice to be made for a project, only to have its findings ignored by the authorities concerned. The Third London Airport inquiry by the Roskill Commission is the classic case of this kind of charade, lasting two and a half years, costing more than a million pounds and producing nine volumes of papers in 1972. It undertook one of the most comprehensive and sophisticated CBAs ever mounted of four short-listed alternative sites. In the event, Stanstead Airport, which was not on the original shortlist, was chosen. Why bother with all that rigorous rigmarole, one is tempted to ask, when governments decide the final outcome by the seat of their pants?

It meant that I had a certain sympathy later when I learned, some time after the event, that the decision to build a third sugar mill in the tiny kingdom of Swaziland, even though I disagreed with it, came about because the businessman with the idea had the ear of the King. At least it saved a lot of time and money on a redundant CBA.

There is a further problem with CBA, if I might climb on another sceptical hobby horse. Arguably, it's based on a philosophical fallacy. CBA is derived from the ideological stable of utilitarianism whose dominant exponent was Jeremy Bentham. In contrast to most philosophers whose main ideas linger on long after their bodies have disintegrated, Bentham's body has been preserved intact, seated fully clothed on a sedan chair in the foyer of University College London, which he founded, even though some of his ideas have all but disappeared. CBA is not one of them, however, and stems from his 'pleasure-pain principle', the idea that moral behaviour can be guided by totting up the pleasures and pains involved in an action and proceeding with it if the pleasures outweigh the pains or, in modern parlance, where the benefits exceed the costs. Bentham devised a 'felicific calculus' for this sum. Herein lies the fallacy. The snag is, pleasures and pains are not additive because they are not qualitatively alike. His second popular idea of seeking 'the greatest happiness of the greatest number' is similarly inadequate as a guide because it's indeterminate. One person may receive greater happiness from an action than the aggregate of several people's individual happiness from the same action assuming, wrongly, that they could be added together.

On this shaky utilitarian philosophical foundation the whole edifice of CBA has been erected. Is it any wonder that its application to projects sends out confusing signals? How do you aggregate qualitatively different benefits and costs and strike a balance? A common illustration of this difficulty is the environmental degradation associated with the construction of a road or a dam. What monetary valuation of a lost view should we put on the cost side of the ledger? It can't be done. All we can do is total the things that can be quantified and exercise judgment as to whether, on balance, the worth of the non-quantifiable aspects is sufficiently significant to warrant changing the initial conclusion to proceed or not with a project.

None of these speculative misgivings about

appraisal procedures, I hasten to add, marred my enjoyment of the sojourn in Saudi Arabia. I acquired a limited hydrological vocabulary and became an engineer for a day when I was lucky enough to experience one of the occasional releases of water from the Malaki Dam during my short stay in the project area. The flow of water is measured in 'cumecs', where one cumec is equal to one cubic metre of water per second. There are 86,400 seconds in a day so if the water flowed at a rate of one cumec all day then 86,400 cubic metres of water would be delivered down the wadi. Since there are 10,000 square metres in one hectare this means that one cumec will water 8.64 hectares of land to a depth of 1 metre in a day.

As the water trickled along the sandy bed of the wadi, various tests were made by the project team to measure the transmission and evaporation losses. Knowing this information and also the volume of water released in millions of cubic metres from the dam enabled estimates of the land area that might be irrigated to be calculated. Clearly, a cumec was a valuable addition to any budding economist's toolkit.

As always, things are a little more complicated than they seem at first sight. The 'water duty' is loosely defined as the amount of water necessary to grow a crop, which is a bit vague. There was much argument between the agriculturalists and the engineers about this. Was it 70 centimetres or nearer 40 to grow dura? Then again, are we talking about the depth of water cover or the depth absorbed into the soil? If the latter, it might require a metre of water on the surface, given the unavoidably heavy losses in sun-baked Saudi Arabia, to get 40 centimetres of penetration into the soil.

All these figures were crucial for estimating the total land area that might be irrigated as a result of the project and its associated potential production.

As luck would have it we were able to gauge the water duty empirically on the day of the water release. After a long day of engineering tests in the field, we wandered back at dusk to the Land Rover. This had been carefully parked on land not due for watering this time under the complicated traditional water rights system of irrigation from the wadi. The importance of this most valuable resource to local farmers had been underlined during the day when we had observed fighting as some farmers sought to 'steal' water out of turn and divert it onto their land with makeshift embankments. As a result we found ourselves in the gathering darkness wading across a field full of water back to the vehicle. I was therefore able to measure the water duty accurately to be the depth of one thigh!

7

Polymania and Academic Games

My return to the City courtesy of Barclays did not last long, ten months in fact. Long enough to research and write a few reports for senior managers and clients, publish a few items in *Barclays Review* and other in-house promotional publications as well as teach on the Friday afternoon 'Economics for Sixth Formers' sessions at the bank's training college in Teddington. One week, the invited school was my own, Latymer, and it gave me a certain *frisson* of excitement expounding the then Conservative government's early flirtation with monetarism to this particular cadre of the intelligentsia whose portals I hadn't managed to penetrate in my own time there as a student.

Ten months was also long enough to realise that Barclays was just a family firm writ large and, like most families, was given to friendly feuding which occasionally broke out into a brawl. Unbeknown to me, a brutal turf war was raging somewhere in the upper reaches of Lombard Street between the UK based 'domestic' bank with its countrywide network of high street branches and the international Barclays DCO, the initials standing for Dominion, Colonial and Overseas – a quaint throwback to past glories. Both had their own group of economists. The newly rationalised structure dictated that they should merge under one umbrella. DCO, transformed into Barclays International, was the winner and among the spoils was the Economic Intelligence Department, much to the chagrin of the longstanding manager and deputy manager of our department. Having lost the battle, they tactfully withdrew from the fray and promptly took early retirement. I left for academia, Oxford Polytechnic to be precise, now in its modern guise renamed even more precisely and definitely more grandly, Oxford Brookes University.

It is a good ploy to apply for education posts after the academic year has started. There may be fewer jobs advertised but this is more than compensated by vastly fewer budding candidates queuing up to offer their services. I saw no sign of the competition. Perhaps they found the job title off-putting: 'Lecturer in Quantitative Economics'. I certainly did. So this is what a buyer's market looks like, I thought. I had a brief meeting (interview was too strong a word for it) with my prospective Head of Department, Dr Horn. Until that time, as one would expect, the academics I had come across had (usually) impressed me with the fluency with which they articulated their views and ideas. They were professional wordsmiths after all. Expectations, however, can sometimes be misleading. I am reminded, for example, of the playwright, Alan Bennett, who when he was contemplating becoming a don, apparently arrived early before giving a lecture to advance the hands of the classroom clock in case he ran out of things to say to his students. Bennett was exceptional in this respect, as was Dr Horn who had a gruff, rasping sort of voice and used words sparingly, if at all. Instead, he confined himself to a rich vocabulary of grunts as his preferred mode of communication. Perhaps other applicants had failed to decipher them. Somehow or other he later managed to distil a few of these into the briefest of offer letters. Then, when I procrastinated over the decision for a few days, weighing up whether to enter higher education or an alternative post in further education, he rang me and barked down the line, 'D'yer want the job or not?' Who could resist such an eloquent invitation?

There was a downside to starting in the middle of an academic year, as I quickly gathered. I should first explain that in those days, the 1970s, before the fashion for modularising everything in sight ricocheted through the groves of academe, social science students followed traditionally structured courses towards an honours degree. They had to pass five subjects in an examination at the end of the first year before proceeding to major in their chosen three subjects examined at the end of the third year.

One of my first tasks was to tutor three of nine seminar groups in the wake of lectures given by a senior colleague in quantitative methods (QM), a first-year compulsory course. After one term's exposure to QM, the students in my groups were climbing up the walls. Most of them were studying social sciences because they regarded themselves as non-numerate and hated mathematics. Perhaps I should have attended the lectures myself but I had enough on my plate picking up the pieces afterwards. Ted was a nice man, in love with his subject, but according to the students spent most of the lecture with his back to them scribbling mathematical hieroglyphics on the board which they found utterly incomprehensible.

I knew where they were coming from. Having taught myself the elements of calculus and matrix algebra from books when I had to, and studied some of the psychology of learning at Dudley College of Education, the word 'motivation' sprang to mind as the nub of the problem. This lot were totally demotivated! What's more, if they survived the first year, they would invariably specialise in law, politics and sociology rather than an economics linked umbilically with QM in their minds. King Canute would have been hard pushed to turn that tide.

For the next few weeks anything resembling a mathematical expression was prohibited. They had to burn out their grievances first, let off steam, and I was the fall guy collecting the flak. Logical argument failed to convince them. I therefore resorted to subterfuge. I preyed on their vested interests. They wanted to concentrate their studies on law, politics or sociology but had a distasteful hurdle to jump first. The rules couldn't be changed in the short run and as we all know from Keynes's dictum, in the long run we're all dead. Trouble is, I told them, they would be metaphorically dead in the short run, too, if they didn't acquire that necessary QM passport to the green pastures of the second year. I appealed to their baser instincts. After all, my reputation was on the line here, too. Since they weren't convinced by the merits of the case for social scientists absorbing a modicum of knowledge about numerate methodologies, I offered them expediency as a motive. Bear the pain for a couple of terms, I told them, and I would drill them with a minimal number of techniques sufficient to pass through the narrow gateway *en route* to nirvana. It worked. The seething stopped and they knuckled down to the work. Most were successful and, dare I say, a few enjoyed the experience and their new-found power. With one or two the bonding was strong enough to last years after they graduated and we are still in touch.

It was something of a baptism by fire and raised recurring questions for my colleagues and me when rethinking the structure of our subject for the sub-mission of a proposal to the Council for National Academic Awards (CNAA). The colonising wave towards modularisation which had been initiated by the Head of the Biology Department with the support of the Director, had swept through Oxpoly, which quickly became a national pioneer in this movement. Within the institution, despite a modicum of resis-tance, it inevitably enveloped the humanities and social sciences. Ostensibly, the task was to formulate an 'economics field' as part of a modular honours degree awarded by the CNAA. The material form of the latter comprised a panel of peer group economists from rival higher education institutions so the real task was to guess the mind of the CNAA. We got it wrong the first time round when other fields had spun the roulette wheel and hit the jackpot. So, the pres-sure was on and the modular office Dean and cavalry arrived to support our second attempt.

Academics thrive on such challenges and are in their element faced with an intensive period of in-depth navel gazing. The situation called for a thorough overhaul of the philosophy of economics. Why do we teach it? What is the 'it' that we're teaching? How do we teach it? Is anyone the wiser when we've taught it? As is well known, economists are the butt of familiar jokes, usually some variant of putting *n* economists together to solve a problem and they will come up with *n + 1* solutions. Ha! Ha! A better version surfaced in an episode of *The West Wing*, the television series on White House politics, when a character said, 'Economists were put on the planet to make astrologers look good.' I like it!

Be that as it may, when a bunch of extra-terrestrial colleagues try to reach a consensus on the heartland of their subject, that's the time to reach for your gun; especially when the outcome of their deliberations has to be collapsed into a limited number of sequential modules on a box diagram representing a coherent field structure. Climbing the north face of the Eiger would feel like a Sunday afternoon stroll by comparison. Intellectual feathers are apt to fly. Professional dignities are trampled on. Ring-fenced chunks of economic territory are liberated. Raw nerves are touched as syllabic old friends are ditched.

A SWOT[9] analysis, if taken at the time, would also have revealed eccentricities in the make-up of the economics team. Keith (History of Economic

---

[9] SWOT is a management tool for making an assessment of an organisation's or team's strengths, weaknesses, opportunities and threats.

Thought), sadly, was deluged with domestic difficulties. With an aged mother in South Wales and a slowly dying girlfriend in Harrogate, much of his life around weekends was spent on trains commuting between them. Consequently, he was unavailable to teach on Mondays and Fridays. Mid-week nights in Oxford found him in a succession of bed and breakfast hostelries accompanied by his portable filing system in a battered leather suitcase along with his laundry. It was a routine somewhat at variance with the notion of staff meetings and agendas held in numbered rooms at set times. There was a much higher probability of running into Keith by accident in the corridor on one of the days when he happened to be around.

Disoriented Julia (Quantitative Methods) had the full panoply of earthy swear words at her disposal and tended to lob aural grenades indiscriminately at anyone within range who dared to cross her. Her alcohol problem fuelled the violence of these onslaughts. Hypochondriacal Paramesh (Economic Analysis) periodically wore a neck brace to remind himself of his condition and never tired of recalling at every meeting that he once did research with one of the gurus of Economics, L.R. Klein. Living in London, he found daily attendance in Oxford problematical. Roy (Industrial Economics), one of the 'Old School', worked like fury all the hours imaginable, burning the midnight oil in search of goals unfathomed by the rest of us.

By this stage, having shed the soubriquet 'Quantitative' from my title, I was revealed in my preferred colours as a development economist: almost the lowest form of life in the hierarchy of the economics profession. As Benjamin Ward made clear in a splendid book, *What's Wrong with Economics?*, if your academic specialism required qualification by an adjective as in, for example, 'economic development', you were beyond the pale. Microeconomics, macroeconomics and econometrics ruled the roost, carried the highest status and were *de rigueur* for anyone planning to make a serious career in the discipline.

A revised minimalist economics field was duly produced after much angst by this strange assemblage of academic life, which passed muster second time around with the CNAA overlords. It had been a sobering experience but why had it been so difficult to chisel out an agreed and acceptable structure? Maybe we were a queer lot but were we so different from other members of the profession? Were our fundamentals being ruthlessly exposed or was it that the subject itself was undergoing some sort of mid-life crisis?

In the course of research for the resubmission it became apparent that there are hidden assumptions underlying the deliberations of any course planning exercise. Firstly, that there is a central core of material which must be acquired by any student of economics. Secondly, what is taught is necessarily what is learned. Thirdly, that the aims of a course of study are in the 'normative' province of 'values' and are therefore separable from its objectives, those aspects dealing with the 'positive' realm of 'facts' which are amenable to measurement. Richard Lipsey, in his *Introduction to Positive Economics*, along with other mainstream economists, seeks to confine the subject to the measurable sphere, emphasising its links with mathematics and the apparent exactness it provides as a way of increasing the subject's scientific credentials.

There may be some mileage in the unreconstructed two-handed economist reviewing these three overlapping issues more closely if only to shed some light on what animates the lecturing fraternity to profess their knowledge, or confess their ignorance, of a particular branch of human creation. In short, what is it that makes us get up in the morning and attempt to speak with conviction on our subject to students? There is of course an enormous temptation to sidestep fundamental questions of what it is one is actually doing as a teacher, dismissing them as woollyminded, liberal excursions which can only lead to unprofitable, inconclusive debate. It is much easier to relapse into the old routine of grinding out a syllabus of 'essential' knowledge and lists of readings under the seductive illusion that such knowledge reflects 'reality' and that students' grasp of economic wisdom can be amply measured by assessment tests of their powers of recall and regurgitation.

As Postman and Weingartner pointed out nearly forty years ago,[10] successive innovations in communications technology makes 'the information dissemination business' in which most teachers are engaged increasingly inappropriate. Reflecting the counter-cultural tendencies of the early 1970s, they claimed that whilst their students were grappling with 'psychology and psychedelics, anthropology and

---

[10] Postman, N. and Weingartner, C. (1971) *Teaching as a Subversive Activity*. Harmondsworth: Penguin, p. 25.

81

anthropomorphism, birth control and biochemistry, their teachers are teaching "subjects" that mostly don't exist any more'. They concluded that 'Teaching is abstract, theoretical, conditioned by a certain conception of knowledge, and divorced from real life'. In a nutshell, the subject occupies a central position, the student a subordinate one.

Let's now add a touch of magic from Carl Rogers to this heady brew of criticism. He contends that 'We cannot teach another person directly; we can only facilitate his learning'.[11] He then describes a typical faculty group planning a new curriculum with its concerns about how much a course should cover, linkages with other programmes, time allocated to certain topics, method of delivery and assessment. All grist-to-the-mill activities instantly recognised by lecturers so engaged and yet, according to Rogers, based on the false hypothesis that what is taught is what is learned.

Moving on from there, Rogers holds that 'A person learns significantly only those things which he perceives as being involved in the maintenance of, or enhancement of, the structure of self'.[12] This suggests that to be actively engaged, a student needs to perceive a problem as a problem or whatever is to be learned as worth learning. This does not preclude the teacher from articulating areas of enquiry but, irrespective of the source, significant learning will only

---

[11] Rogers, Carl R. (1965) *Client-centered Therapy*. Boston, MA: Houghton Mifflin, p. 389.
[12] ibid.

take place if the learner perceives the enquiry as relevant.

Furthermore, evidence from the field of transactional psychology seems to show that our perceptions do not come from things around us but from within us and that they are largely a function of our previous experiences, assumptions and needs. These perceptions will not change until actions based on them fail to work in the sense of fulfilling our purposes. Hence learning is seen as the process of relinquishing inappropriate perceptions and developing more workable ones. Since each individual's perception will be unique, communication is only possible to the extent that two perceivers have similar purposes and share common experiences and assumptions. Perceptions are standardised in language categories and in a sense we 'see' with our language. That the same event may be perceived differently by people is evidenced by their different actions in response to it.

The implications of these findings are far-reaching. They indicate that people assign their own meanings to their observations and experiences. The division between an inner subjective world and an outer objective one would appear to be artificial and leads to 'the "fallacy of misplaced concreteness" in which a higher degree of external "reality" is assigned to the abstracted aspects of experience than to the total experience from which they are abstracted'.[13] This line of reasoning points to the notion that there is no

---

[13] The fallacy is attributed to A.N. Whitehead in Heaton, J.M. (1968) *The Phenomenology and Psychology of Function and Disorder*. London: Pitman Medical Publishing.

such thing as 'subject matter' in the abstract, although institutional practice often casts the student in the role of a receiver of a subject's canon of objective knowledge. If knowledge is what we know after we have learned and is derived from perception, then it will be unique and subjective like any other perception. It is therefore difficult to escape the conclusion that a student-centred curriculum is not only desirable but logically the only option.

There is more. If the educational aim is in some sense to produce a 'good' economist, evaluative terms would have to be used in defining the objectives necessary to achieve this aim – careful observation of the facts, correct interpretation of economic relationships, skilful analysis of problems, shrewd exercise of judgement – because prescriptive statements can only be analysed in prescriptive terms. But objectives are supposedly value-free, describing acts of behaviour capable of being demonstrated after studying a subject, such as the ability to perform certain skills. Hence achieving objectives cannot add up to achieving an aim because prescriptive value statements cannot be derived from descriptive factual statements. Thus, economics cannot be just confined to the sphere of what 'is' and revealed in technical skills. It has to dirty its hands in the murky world of what 'ought to be' and express opinions and judgements on policies to get there. It is quintessentially 'normative' rather than 'positive' – 'political economy' as opposed to 'economic science'.

By this stage you may well be thinking he's lost the plot! Economics has virtually disappeared over the horizon, buried in a sea of semantics. I would retaliate that it's not much good waxing eloquent on the properties of an elegant linear programming model of the economy if your students are making a bee-line for the door. We are in the learning business and the higher education audience is no longer captive. It votes with its feet. For that reason I would argue that we are also perforce in the entertainment business, faced with the challenge of seeing that students don't leave the performance before the interval.

The authors cited above made it clear that if we were sailing between the Scylla of a subject-centred approach and the Charybdis of the student-centred approach, the ship of learning should veer towards shipwreck on the latter rather than the former. The poly's think-tank of economists was not ready to be so bold, and despite a spate of books of the ilk, *What's Wrong with Lectures?* could not bring themselves to accept the disquieting and revolutionary words of Ivan Illich in his book *Deschooling Society* that 'most learning requires no teaching'. Instead we had devised an economics field with the slightly modernised, conventional 80/20 structure: 80 per cent prescribed content and 20 per cent student-chosen assignment.

This exercise confirmed my growing impression that there was no purist, objective, mantle of economics 'out there' for all followers to imbibe but a series of ideas and perceptions put forward by writers in the field committed to various beliefs and positions which they sought to promote among their peers and society at large. Let us indulge in a bit of history of the development of economics to make the point.

We have already touched on Adam Smith (1723–90)

85

in Chapter 4. One of his preoccupations was trying to find an explanation for the different prices at which goods exchanged in markets. The search began with the idea of *value* as the possible foundation on which prices rest. Smith observed that goods may possess two different types of value: 'value in use' or 'value in exchange'. Some goods such as water might have great value in use but little exchange value in the sense that hardly anything else could be exchanged for it. A not very useful good like a diamond, however, has a high exchange value because lots of things could be purchased in exchange for it. What then causes the value of goods?

In a famous example describing a hunting society, Smith suggests that if it usually takes twice the labour to kill a beaver than to kill a deer then one beaver should exchange for two deer. He concludes that the produce of two days' or two hours' labour should be worth twice the produce of one day's or one hour's labour. In such a society the whole produce belongs to the labourer and hence labour is the source of value. Smith's Labour Theory of Value was later developed and used to devastating effect by Karl Marx to unravel what he saw as the inequities produced by capitalism.

Smith records that:

As soon as the land of any country has all become private property the landlords, like all other men, love to reap where they never sowed, and demand a rent even for its natural produce ... As soon as stock has accumulated in the hands of particular persons, some of them will naturally employ it in setting to work industrious people, whom they will supply with materials and subsistence, in order to make a profit by the sale of their work, or by what their labour adds to the value of the materials.[14]

This raises a new question. If labour is the sole creator of value what is the justification for property rents and profits? A cloud descends on the argument. Smith, in the passage above, as a realist simply asserts their existence. His main concern is to create the best conditions for increasing output which will improve the country's prosperity. The accumulation of capital is done by capitalists out of their profits. Free trade is advocated by Smith to increase the size of the market for industrial products. This will enable more specialisation to occur in industry leading to higher levels of output. He considers the best environment for this process to flourish is one in which competition exists and the market rather than the state regulates trading transactions.

In short, Smith's analysis serves his desire to promote prosperity by increasing production which in turn requires free trade and markets. That's the axe he is grinding. Not much fence-sitting there.

Likewise, David Ricardo (1772–1823), in the course of unsuccessfully searching for some absolute standard for measuring the value of output, spots that the ratio of profits to wages in commodity prices will vary according to the ratio of capital to labour used in

---

[14] Quoted in Robinson, J. (1962) *Economic Philosophy*. Harmondsworth: Penguin, p. 32.

producing the commodities. The more capital involved, the bigger the share of funds from the sale of its output going to profits. Labour's share, wages, will correspondingly be smaller. This reasoning was used, in time, as the justification for profits on the implicit grounds that capital must also be creating value. The idea that labour is the only source of value is therefore abandoned in the central economic tradition.

Thomas Malthus (1766–1835) worried about the population effects of increasing output. He thought population growth as prosperity increased would outstrip food production. It was reduced, however, by 'preventive checks', preferably in the form of moral restraint such as late marriage or, more darkly, and I quote, by 'Promiscuous intercourse, unnatural passions, violations of the marriage bed, and improper arts to conceal the consequences of irregular con-nexions'[15] – in a word, vice. Population growth would also be held back by 'positive checks' such as wars, famine and disease. Both sorts of checks operating together, many of them deriving from the scarcity of food supplies and poverty, meant that in consequence most people would be forced to live at subsistence level. Malthus could not foresee the dramatic increa-ses in production heralded by the agricultural and industrial revolutions which soon negated his views on population. They may be dead but they refuse to lie down and their ghost is often seen stalking the

---

[15] Malthus, T.R. (1826) *An Essay on the Principle of Population*, 6th edn. London: John Murray, pp. 4-17.

poverty-induced famines prevalent in many developing countries.

Ricardo shared this view to the extent that land could not be increased in line with the rising wealth of the nation. In consequence, landowners would benefit by raising rents depending on the quality of their land, as land became more scarce. Rent would be a deduction from the value of output produced and capitalists and workers would divide the rest between them. He claimed that 'Every rise of profits is favourable to the accumulation of capital, and to the increase of population, and therefore would, in all probability, ultimately lead to an increase in rent'.[16]

Thus, profits are necessary for capital and output to increase. The latter encourages population to grow, pressing harder on the available land for food production, leading to higher rents for the landlords. In Galbraith's words, 'capitalists must prosper if there is to be progress and landlords cannot help reaping its fruits'.[17] For the rest, their position is summarised by Ricardo:

> Labour, like all other things which are purchased and sold, and which may be increased or diminished in quantity, has its natural and its market price which is necessary to enable the labourers, one with another, to subsist and perpetuate their race, without increase or diminution.[18]

---

[16] Quoted in Galbraith, J.K. (1958) *The Affluent Society*. Harmondsworth: Penguin, p. 34.

[17] ibid.

[18] ibid.

In other words, subsistence-level wages are likely to prevail in many societies, especially if the number seeking employment out of the population grows at a faster rate than the number of jobs being created by employers, the owners of capital.

This Cook's Tour of some of the key ideas of the early giant economists suggests that whilst they may have been great analysts they were also strong advocates for their favoured positions. Collectively, they and others writing in a similar vein are known as the 'classical economists', so called because their analysis was based on the division of English society into the three major social classes – workers, capitalists and landlords – and sought to explain the distribution of income between them in the form of wages, profits and rents. Is it just an accident that the theories setting prices and wages in their classical economic system created such huge differences between the rewards earned by labour and their abject living conditions of hardship and poverty and the rewards gained by capitalists and rentiers affording them a privileged existence of leisure and luxury? As Galbraith remarks, 'generally the classical tradition was reticent on the subject of power'.[19]

Armed with these historical revelations I became less concerned about maintaining a painful, intellectual balance between competing economic doctrines reviewed with equal objectivity and impartiality. I recalled that John Stuart Mill in his *Autobiography*, when experiencing a mental crisis, had written that

---

[19] Galbraith, J.K. (1989) *A History of Economics*. Harmondsworth: Penguin, p. 115.

'the habit of analysis has a tendency to wear away the feelings'.[20] Likewise, an old Kierkegaard quote, always worth dropping out at cocktail parties, affirms that 'the sclerosis of objectivity is the annihilation of existence'. Musing on these inspirational words, I felt better. I wanted an economics to advocate with a degree of passion. I started doing my own thing. Being a one-handed economist no longer held fears as I realised, belatedly, that the profession had been stuffed full of them since its earliest days.

---

[20] Mill, J.S. (1873) *Autobiography*, in M. Lerner (ed.) (1961) *Essential Works of John Stuart Mill*. New York: Bantam Books, p. 85.

8

Swazi Interludes

At some point, the polytechnic recognised that its engineering origins, with a penchant for locking students in classrooms for thirty hours a week in order to cover the syllabus, was not the best way to promote efficient learning. Many lecturers had had no professional training. Partly to plug this gap an Educational Methods Unit was established, headed by an innovative educationist with some modest resource grants to finance staff release time, enabling a member of staff to develop a new methodological approach to their work. I was in there like a flash and secured the first award even though I had entered the profession via the teacher training college route.

The problem was this. The take-up on my first year, first term, Introduction to Economics module had grown to two hundred students. There was no way I could handle such numbers with the traditional Oxford style lecture-seminar-tutorial weekly sandwich. In the era of higher education expenditure cuts, allocating more staff from the small economics team was not an option given that only around thirty students would continue with economics, the rest taking it as a prerequisite module for other fields of study.

The solution was hardly original since I stole it from the Open University. I hadn't been one of their part-time tutors for nothing! It was only radical within the confines of the polytechnic environment. Seminars and tutorials were abandoned because they were staff intensive. Lectures were retained because they were not. The release time was used to write five study booklets as a guided reading programme emphasising a 'learning by doing' approach with activities and self-assessment tasks. A chunk of time was set aside for weekly 'surgeries' when students with problems could come and discuss them. Those who were coping with the work, many of whom already had an A-level in economics and were taking it as a soft module, never appeared at all. One-to-one sessions with students coming fresh to a new subject and therefore not having much to say, far from being like a football match where the tutor initiated all the moves, made all the passes and scored all the goals, suddenly became alive and interesting because they started from students' problems.

Was it a cheat to introduce an element of distance learning in an institutional setting? Maybe, but it was the only way I could think of for dealing with this particular problem which was both educational and economic in nature. The solution to the latter did at any rate seek to optimise the use of scarce staff resources, namely mine, which is the operational territory for an economist and it was pleasing to note that some other fields adopted a similar approach.

On the status front there was a more serious constraint. Passage to 'senior lecturer' had been fairly
automatic but the real logjam was the next step to
principal lecturer. I never quite fathomed this out. It
appeared to be closely akin to choosing a new Pope
and one half-expected the announcement of a new
principal lecturer to be preceded by an emission of
white smoke so rarely did they occur. I once imagined
how Laurie Taylor might depict the process in what
was then his regular column in the *Times Higher
Education Supplement*. Perhaps something like the
following . . .

Chairman:	Well, as you know, this year's Advancement Committee is not meeting in the most propitious circumstances in view of the cuts, etc. and it goes without saying that we all have to be even more ruthlessly objective than usual about the merits of the thirty candidates for principal lecturer. You all have the papers in front of you, I believe?
Dean, Technology:	Could I ask if there's a ceiling figure?
Chairman:	Hm . . . er . . . not in so many words but let's just say that the fingers of one hand should cover it. In fact, on this point and just to ease our task a little, I did suggest that the five Deans might rank applications from

their respective faculties ordin-
ally, earmarking their most
favoured candidate with an 'A'
and so on. This short-circuiting
of our work will, of course, in
no way prejudice our final
selection. All thirty names put
forward by heads of department will have an equal chance
of being drawn out of the hat,
so to speak, based on their
performance under the usual
criteria, teaching profile,
research and administration.
We are searching scientifically
for the outstanding among the
brilliant, for the charismatic
communicator, pioneering
scholar and creative manager all
rolled into one.

Staff rep: Jesus Christ!

Chairman: An excellent model, Mr T., if I
may say so. Perhaps we can
now open the bidding and
move to a discussion of each
faculty's hopefuls beginning
with technology.

Dean, If I might start the ball rolling,
Engineering: Chairman, I was just curious to
know why Dr P. Kherani, BA
(Cantab), MSc (London), PhD
(Stanford), D Phil (Oxon), who
on the face of it seems to be

96

quite a strong candidate with forty-nine articles and two books to his credit, Chief Examiner for the Chartered Institute of Engineers, fifteen years uninterrupted service on the Academic Board and an acknowledged expert in educational technology, has been passed over yet again for the tenth time?

Dean, Technology: Quite simple, really. He's weak on two grounds. Firstly, he's got the wrong handshake. Secondly, his habit of teaching in Gujarati tends to irritate the students.

Dean, Engineering: Oh, I see ...

That's enough of that! Meanwhile, back in the real world, my spoor was being tracked by the scout of a new tribe, well, new to me. A headhunter was on my trail. Polytechnic life in Oxford was, in a sense, too comfortable if your specialist focus is on the economic development of poor countries but paradoxically, too uncomfortable if, Micawber-like, annual outgoings exceed annual income. Consequently, I had been firing off enquiries looking for alternative openings. The headhunter recruitment consultant must have been on the end of one of these investigatory salvos and invited me to an initial meeting at the Naval and Military Club in Piccadilly. Over the coffee and sugar crystals, we discussed the possibility of joining the Commonwealth Development Corporation (CDC) as Principal of the Mananga Agricultural Management Centre (MAMC) in Swaziland. A second interview was arranged with senior executives of CDC at their offices in Mayfair, and a final one with CDC's Regional Controller in southern Africa who was on a visit to the UK sealed my fate. By an unexpected route I was getting promotion to a different sort of principal after all.

As it happens, I was already familiar with Swaziland. In the late 1970s I had previously escaped from the comfort zone of Oxford on secondment for two years as one of ODA's technical co-operation officers loosely attached to Swaziland's Ministry of Education as their Education Planning Research Adviser. I say loosely because the Ministry was located in Mbabane, the capital, and the job was located nearly thirty miles away and about two thousand feet lower, at the Kwaluseni campus of the university near the commercial centre of Manzini.

It emerged later that there was no love lost between the Ministry and the university, if only because the latter absorbed over 20 per cent of the total education budget, strove for autonomy and declined to accept the government's strictures in favour of policy-oriented research relevant to its development initiatives. Reporting to a boss in both camps meant falling into the gulf between these two postures was an inevitable occupational hazard. Almost from day one the arguments began. Why should the university allocate a house from its scarce stock to this man from the Ministry when he wasn't doing any lecturing? It was an inauspicious beginning which required intervention by the British High Commission to resolve.

The physical separation involved fairly frequent commuting between Manzini and Mbabane. Apart from the high risk of being run off the road by the taxis plying between the two towns, this was a spectacular journey. The sensuous delight in descending below 'Sheba's Breasts', the twin peaks flanking the route snaking down from the high veldt, remains firmly stored in the memory and did much to allay the tetchiness flavouring the meetings at either end.

Although the list of duties represented about ten years' work, in the event it boiled down to two entirely different tasks. These were to design and implement from scratch a school-leaver tracer project funded by the World Bank and to initiate activities in the Faculty of Education's dormant and staffless department, The Swaziland Institute for Educational Research.

After the preliminary work of assembling a small army of research assistants, designing survey documents and acquiring a project vehicle, fieldwork for the tracer project involved careering around the Swazi countryside with an intrepid band of young researchers hunting down erstwhile school-leavers and firing questions at them. Swaziland is about the size of Wales, even more mountainous and with some place names echoing the Welsh double 'll' pronunciation. The detective work usually began at the secondary school attended by a leaver identified in the sample, each one of which was visited, taking the team to every part of the country.

Much can be gleaned about the problems of development from visual impressions and some of the absurdities of remedial interventions. In remoter rural areas, for instance, school classrooms would be sparsely furnished, have cardboard windows and the pupils taught by fledgling teachers just out of college struggling to survive let alone manage educational innovations. In this environment two of the crazier improvement initiatives witnessed were projects by the British Council and the World Bank. With the best of intentions the British Council had supplied each secondary school with an equipment package designed to improve the teaching of science. Ostensibly a good idea at first glance, its effect in practice rather soured the initial impression. We learned that some head teachers had sold the stuff and others, for fear it would be broken, kept it safely away from pupils in a store under lock and key. Where the instruments and equipment had been utilised there was no budgetary provision for covering the inevitable breakages. Someone hadn't done their homework.

The second case was even more bizarre. In the middle of nowhere it seemed, on one of the journeys, we suddenly came across this magnificent, modern structure annexed to a school. It transpired that this was a World Bank concept for dual use of the premises by schoolchildren and members of the local farming community. The modernised bit consisted of a workshop fully equipped with power tools and benches so that farmers could come in and mend their fences and rural buildings. The only snag was that the school had no electricity, nor running water for that matter. Perhaps that was why it was deserted on the day we chanced upon it. Apparently, several of these 'white elephants' were planned for around the country. It brought to mind old film shots of a six-lane motorway in Ghana at the time of Dr Nkrumah along which goats were being herded without a car in sight. Both examples ignore Albert Hirschman's view that this kind of expensive infrastructure development entailing long-term recurrent maintenance and running costs should be demand, not supply, driven so that a dirt road is only tarred, for example, when it's clogged with traffic.

On one of these safaris chasing school-leavers in the sugar-growing low veldt, I unwittingly glimpsed the future. Chancing across the signboard at the entrance to the campus of the MAMC and not having heard of its existence before, I made an impromptu visit and had a brief conversation with one of the English management trainers. I remember being impressed with the facilities and the location and thinking this would be a pleasant place to work but had no inkling that six years later events would conspire to make this a reality.

The report on the tracer project was wound up back in Oxford and eventually published under the title *From School ... To Work* and probably disappeared without trace. The Swaziland Institute for Educational Research was left with a slightly higher profile after a series of seminar programmes at the university, presented by various development specialists and project managers working throughout Swaziland, led to the launch of the *SIER Bulletin* to publish their findings.

My return for a second stint in Swaziland afforded an opportunity to manage a very different sort of project. The MAMC was an international, residential management training centre established by the CDC in 1972 offering post-experience management development programmes to middle and senior managers working on projects and in a variety of development institutions in their own countries. Mainstay courses focused on managerial and organisational behaviour and resource management, particularly financial accounting and budgetary control, interspersed with specialist programmes on project management, food policy management, computer management, rural credit management and the management of irrigation projects. Participants came predominantly from East, Central and West African countries but also from the Caribbean, Papua New Guinea, Bangladesh, Nepal, Fiji and the Solomon Islands so that each course contained an exciting cauldron of nationalities.

Almost uniquely among training institutions in sub-Saharan Africa, each course member had a single en suite study bedroom and enjoyed a high standard of catering and recreational facilities including an excellent restaurant, swimming pool, bar, common room and sports fields. The campus provided a comfortable retreat appropriate for experienced personnel to think about their work situation and engage in a free exchange of problems and ideas with others from around the world facing similar managerial concerns. They were together for three to nine weeks depending on the course.

What a development laboratory! Twenty or thirty development practitioners working in ministries of agriculture, on rural development projects, in commercial banks, at research institutions, in private plantation companies, on irrigation schemes or with non-governmental organisations (NGOs), some with responsibility for large numbers of staff, gathered at Mananga to learn how to manage their organisations more effectively.

For the one-handed advocate, what a canvas to paint on! Here was the raw material, the leaven in the lump, with the potential to effect dramatic improvements in all sorts of development contexts. If the Centre's training team got it right, our experienced managers on course, wielding considerable influence in their respective organisations back home, would make transforming waves on their return, rippling through a large number of economically less developed countries. The impact on productive output, and the growth in incomes and prosperity, would be substantial. But let's not get carried away. That little word 'if' three sentences back hides a multitude of sins. What does 'getting it right' really mean? Harking back several decades to the early years after independence it would have meant hordes of well-meaning European development missionaries telling the inhabitants of former colonies how to improve their agriculture, overlooking the thesis well argued by Theodore Schultz[21] that several centuries of practice had made indigenous farmers economically efficient operators given the existing resources and techniques at their disposal.

---

[21] Schultz, T.W. (1964) *Transforming Traditional Agriculture*. New Haven, CT: Yale University Press, p. 37.

Tutors at the Centre liked to think that we were less arrogant than that. Yet despite individual differences in background and experience there was a sort of collective vision on offer and I suppose advocated in a semi-unconscious way. It was transmitted via the structure of the management development programmes and was summed up in what came to be known as the 'Mananga Experience'. It consisted of providing course members with ample opportunity to examine their own managerial experience on the grounds that learning has more to do with re-organising this experience than acquiring fresh facts or principles from outside. The training team's role was to provide an environment which enabled managers to confront their problems and 'critical incidents' at work and the way in which they exercised their responsibilities. They could then reassess their actions and behaviour within the supportive yet critically constructive framework of a group of peers facing similar situations. In the process, course members gained fresh insights and new perceptions, enhancing their confidence as managers to the benefit of both themselves and their organisations. One of the fascinating aspects to emerge from this exercise was the revelation that despite vast differences in context and culture between participants' countries around the world there nevertheless appeared to be a certain commonality in the kind of problems that they were handling. Inevitably the bulk of these involved inter-personal relationships and communications.

Were we successful in our endeavours to assist managers to become more effective? Only their bosses, organisations and the recipients of their services could really say for there was no way the Centre could systematically find out. There were, however, some straws in the wind. To a large extent we had to rely on the market. If there was a consistently good response to our promotional activities in the form of a steady demand for our training programmes and plenty of repeat business from client organisations, then arguably we must be doing something right. Frequently, that was the main guide other than a self-selected group of alumni who would kindly write complimentary letters and let us know how they were getting on since their course with implementing the action plans they clutched when departing from Mananga. A similar correspondence arose with satis-fied employers.

There was also our own professional post-mortems among the staff, fed by the 'happiness sheets' completed by each participant at the end of their stay, which helped to improve the structure and content of future programmes. We generally had a pretty good idea anyway of what had worked well and what had gone belly up. In my time, the only occasion that a course really ploughed was in relation to one already in the pipeline before I arrived and exceptionally directed by an outside consultant from a high-powered European agricultural research institution. In his final appraisal speech he proceeded to blame everything that had gone wrong on the host's inputs and attrib-uted to himself all the successful features. In the light of that sobering event I resolved that MAMC staff would provide the course director on all future pro-grammes. Interestingly, this hapless experience occurred with the highest academically qualified intake of any MAMC course for a management of agricultural research programme. Members, without exception, were specialist scientists managing research stations with at least a masters degree and included a fair number with PhDs. They found Mananga's participatory facilitation techniques anathema, particularly in organisational behaviour, so conditioned were they to formal lecture-centred methods still dominant in African universities.

Course monitoring meetings reviewing feedback and our intuitive feel for gauging the mood of participants played a part in watching the progress of a course. Nine weeks was a long time for managers to be off the job and away from home. Inevitably there was a dip around the middle of each programme which we tried to offset with off-campus training visits, weekend trips to Manzini and Mbabane, sports days and structured programmes with planned activities building towards goals and climaxes. Understandably, some course members suffering privations in their own countries arrived in Swaziland clutching empty suitcases to return home with various goodies acquired from shopping expeditions. Others were undoubtedly benefiting from financial *per diems* during training to supplement meagre Civil Service salaries. Yet despite these motivations, in my judgement, most of the managers who attended MAMC's programmes gained some new insight and extra confidence to cope with their managerial problems back on the job.

There was another major indicator of Mananga's credibility as a training institution. CDC, I soon learned, was rather schizophrenic about MAMC's very existence. One strand within the corporation, the 'accountants', wondered why this loss-making project was allowed to continue in CDC's portfolio with its commercial orientation, albeit in high-risk investment schemes in LDCs. CDC was then bailing out MAMC's deficits to the tune of £300,000–£450,000 annually. The other strand, the 'developers', recognised the valuable if unquantifiable role that MAMC played as a kind of flagship public relations project serving in a small way the training needs of managers from agricultural organisations in Africa and other countries around the world in which CDC was operating. For them the kudos gained by the corporation therefore wholly justified MAMC's subsidy.

Against this scenario, unbeknown to me and about the time I joined, CDC's General Manager, Sir Peter Meinertzhagen, had approached the President of the World Bank, Mr Tom Clausen, with an informal request for the Bank to review MAMC's role and make recommendations for its future development. As a result, towards the end of my first year, under the auspices of the Economic Development Institute (EDI), a high-powered seven-man World Bank team, larger than Mananga's staff faculty, breezed into our mountain retreat like a whirlwind to investigate our activities. It was an invigorating and exhausting experience. Anyone who's faced a third degree at the hands of Bob Youker, then EDI's management training specialist, reaching for his ninth in a broadside of questions while one is still stuttering an answer to the first one will understand what I mean. Their invasion was both stimulating and instructive and it was a particular pleasure for me that the Bank's missionaries were headed by J. Price Gittinger, whose book, *Economic Analysis of Agricultural Projects* was a favourite of mine during my teaching career.

In addition to their onslaught of interrogations at Mananga, members of the team had begun their enquiries with senior managers of CDC in London, and after their few days in Swaziland dispersed to visit various African countries, taking soundings from MAMC's client organisations and former course participants. They reassembled in Harare in December 1985 to finalise their report. It was good to learn that top of their list of findings was confirmation of our own impressions that the MAMC 'style' of teaching was very effective. All the team's conversations with organisations and alumni indicated that after training at Mananga managers had gained confidence and were much better at working with their staff. They also underlined that there was considerable demand for such training and strong support from the donor community.

Not all their findings were so positive. They found MAMC to be isolated both physically and intellectually. Relative remoteness we could live with, knowing that the caricature of World Bank consultants on the hoof is that they view anywhere an hour and a quarter away from the airport – the journey time from Matsapha to Mananga – as equivalent to penetrating the Amazon jungle. Intellectual isolation, however, was a more telling criticism. What they really meant was that staff were cut off from outside collegiate contact with other institutions and government agencies because they were too heavily programmed with continuous teaching loads throughout the year. That was a fair point and meant that it was harder to keep abreast of the latest management thinking pioneered at the frontiers of research. Since we were not trying to ape the Harvard Business School, and the team had satisfied themselves that MAMC'c training methods worked, some of the sting of this criticism had been drawn.

We bought into most of the team's findings in the subsequent months, by creating time for a more outward-looking approach and establishing Mananga Consultancy Services for this purpose, offering training and consultancy in client organisations' own countries. The process of internationalising senior staff to get away from an obvious neo-colonial image was begun with the recruitment of new members of staff from Ghana, Ethiopia and Zimbabwe and the team's recommendation to develop a Portuguese language capability in view of Mozambique's and Angola's membership of the Southern African Development Coordination Conference (SADCC) group of countries, was partially implemented by appointing a Portuguese-speaking librarian.

The overall impact of the World Bank Review Mission had been very encouraging, setting pathways for future development and generating a certain amount of excitement among the Mananga staff about aspiring to new goals. This focus on taking stock of the Centre's operations led to other considerations. Whilst the World Bank report meant that we could take some pride in the fact that Mananga's work was worthwhile and seemed to be appreciated by its recipients, this did not remove the bottom line red figures from the institution's annual accounts nor ward off the suspected opponents of financially non-performing projects within CDC's head office. I was also aware from meetings with other directors of training institutions in Africa of the importance of financial viability. For them it was essential in order to escape complete reliance on government handouts which were increasingly difficult to obtain, but more broadly, it was also an appropriate strategy for any organisation seeking to develop greater autonomy and the ability to branch into new activities such as research and consultancy. A benign parent body like CDC might not remain generous indefinitely.

It did not take many hours with the accounts to discover the financial Achilles heel in MAMC's operations. On campus, Mananga had thirty-five single study bedrooms and most of these were occupied during core programmes. To break even and cover all the Centre's costs, however, I calculated that we needed over fifty managers in attendance, a number way in excess of our capacity. This was crazy economics and my instincts as a one handed-economist were rapidly turning capitalistic as I began to realise some of the problems faced by hoteliers. I had often been puzzled how the multi-storey Carlton Hotel in Johannesburg, for instance, managed to remain open when at one time it rarely had any rooms occupied above the fourth floor. Clearly it must have been doing something right.

The idea of reducing costs, most of which were senior staff costs including a substantial overhead charged by head office on all its projects and those of the over ninety local support staff, had little appeal. The World Bank had recommended a modest increase in faculty staff and laying off local workers would have had an adverse effect on the local economy and led to considerable individual hardship. Reducing costs would have been tantamount to reducing the quality of services offered by MAMC in respect of effective management training in comfortable well-resourced facilities. These formed the basis of its reputation and the source of its continued popularity. For these reasons a cost-cutting approach was rejected.

What about course fees? At first glance one was bound to hesitate about raising fees when MAMC training was already regarded as relatively expensive. On the other hand ... Whoops! Almost slipped into dual-handedness mode again. What I really meant to say was that a deeper look at the situation suggested that none of the beneficiaries of MAMC's training paid their own fees. All of them had some form of sponsorship either from their ministry, company, international funding agency such as the British Council, or from bursaries offered by MAMC from block grants made to us from donor organisations. Furthermore, there was a strong and continuing demand from client organisations which, arguably, was relatively inelastic and, due to the mechanisms of sponsorship, would be fairly insensitive to price changes.

For these reasons I advocated to colleagues and CDC's senior management that we should aim at a break-even occupancy rate of 80 per cent which meant that every participant in excess of twenty-eight in attendance would contribute to an element of surplus revenue over costs. This would necessitate an increase in fees which could be partly shaded by reducing the length of core programmes. In turn this would create scope for increasing the number of programmes offered and introducing outreach consultancy services. The strategy, after some initial misgivings, was accepted by my head office overlords and its successful implementation was well under way at the time of my departure from Swaziland in 1988 with MAMC proposing its first break-even budget. That should keep the accountants' wing of CDC at bay for a while, I thought.

There is a sad postscript to this chapter which is difficult to understand. By the late 1990s CDC had decided that Mananga was not part of its core business and would be closed. It had tried unsuccessfully to interest other parties in taking over the Centre, notably the Crown Agents which had a management contract to run it for two or three years, and the Swaziland government. I visited Mananga in April 1998 and met Dr Taruvinga, the last remaining member of the senior staff faculty, who was endeavouring to run courses with a group of associates as a private company pending the establishment of a secondary school on the campus. Most of the facilities were in mothballs and housing and other buildings were slowly deteriorating for lack of maintenance, and only a skeleton local staff remained.

At the time, I was working in neighbouring South Africa on a European Union (EU) funded public service management development project where one of the key training providers, the South African Management Development Institute, was operating without a residential facility from a couple of floors in separate high-rise office blocks in the centre of Pretoria. The irony was inescapable. Management was

identified as a major constraint on African development in nearly every evaluation report by donor
agencies on the continent's problems. Yet in Swaziland, which at that time held the training brief on
behalf of the SADC countries in the southern Africa
region, a magnificent residential, purpose-built, management training centre was being abandoned and
turned into a local secondary school to save sugar
estate managers from sending their children to private
schools in South Africa. Whatever the circumstances
that brought it about, this was a crass decision. As a
former principal who had spent three years working
with staff colleagues to preserve and build upon
MAMC's reputation in the vital field of management
development, I was moved to write a letter to the
Secretary of State of the Department for International
Development, Clare Short, urging her to prevent the
implementation of this decision. It was never
answered. CDC's bean counters had had the last laugh
after all.

Worse was to come if reports in the *Financial
Times* were to be believed.[22] Written by Cathy New-
man, the *FT*'s Chief Political Correspondent, they
spotlighted parliamentary criticisms of CDC's transformation into CDC Capital Partners as a stepping
stone towards full privatisation and the shedding of its
traditional role as a development agency in the process. Using low interest Treasury funds, CDC had
offered long-term assistance with capital, know-how
and management expertise, mainly to fairly risky
agricultural projects in poor countries aiming to

---

[22] *Financial Times*, 2, 4, 5, 6 August 2002.

achieve modest returns of around 8 per cent. In its new guise as a private equity fund, the critics claimed, it was selling out its traditional investments in agriculture in order to make 25 per cent returns in profitable rich-country industries such as telecoms, banks, minerals, oil, gas and property.

An earlier article in *The Economist*[23] was equally forthright, declaring that under its new configuration of CDC Capital Partners around two-thirds of the staff had been laid off, most of them agricultural experts in small African countries, and CDC was closing its offices in Uganda, Malawi and Ghana. Such moves were in direct conflict with the poverty alleviation policy of the Department for International Development, CDC's only shareholder and therefore owner. For the year ending 31 December 2001, according to the *FT*, CDC's investments had plunged and it was making negative returns of 10.3 per cent. The proposed privatisation of CDC had been shelved, the Chief Executive had quit and its future was very much in doubt since the restructuring exercise was not succeeding and it had already laid off experienced staff which would make recovering its earlier developmental role virtually impossible.

---

[23] *The Economist*, 31 December 2001, p. 90.

9

The View From Tank Hill

*My first freelance assignment was back in Uganda.
The following lines were penned in late 1988 after
the mayhem of Idi Amin's and Milton Obote's second administration had finally collapsed. Yoweri
Museveni assumed power as President in 1986.*

I had always thought of myself as an 'institution man',
not really fancying the role of an independent, itinerant, expatriate consultant. A lot of them passed
through the doors of my last post in Swaziland. They
are a special breed but I did not envy them their
transient existence. But circumstances change and
here I am back in Uganda for a few months where I
first caught the 'development bug' over twenty years
ago in the now halcyon days of the 1960s.

Tank Hill is not the best vantage point from which
to renew acquaintances. The name has no military
significance. It is not, for instance, where Amin launched his attack on the Kabaka's palace in 1966 during
President Obote's first period in office. Soon after
independence in 1962, however, it did earn a certain

notoriety as the scene of a wild party with British expatriates play-acting the 'White Man's Burden' in a manner offensive to the host government. No, the tank in question is for water. Not that the hill doesn't have a touch of the fortress about it or at any rate the houses which are usually owned by wealthy Ugandans and let to visiting outsiders – diplomats, aid personnel, multinational executives, Church missionaries and even consultants.

Inequalities somehow always seem that much more stark and incongruous in LDCs and the seven-bedroom, three-bathroom house in which I temporarily reside is part of that incongruity. An inordinate amount of time is spent switching on and off security lights floodlighting approaches to the house and in locking and unlocking iron-barred doors marking its various entrances, not to mention the solid cast-iron gates with spikes on top at the threshold of the drive. Residual gunfire on some nights, setting off a chorus of unseen barking dogs that patrol the compounds, is a reminder of the turmoil of the last two decades and the reason for the fortifications.

Tank Hill, surmounted by the Hotel Diplomate with its latter-day Ugandan Jim Reeves crooning to the diners, is an artificial cul de sac: a real estate repository for individual wealth made in the city. Reality, for most of the urban population of Kampala, starts below – in Kabalagala, for example, humming with evening commuters returning from the city threading their way through an army of vendors selling anything from plastic sachets of milk and freshly caught Nile perch and tilapia from Lake Victoria to soya bean samosas and charcoal-cooked meat. Small *dukas* (shops) lining the road reflect their position on the fringe of affluence with freezer-stocked foods – chicken, cheese, butter and bacon – imported from Kenya, French wines, Scotch whiskies and, in one case, a video film library. Pavement cafés afford conversation places for international sojourners during the daytime and all-night discos at weekends. A unisex hair salon stands nearby. Covered market stalls offer pyramids of fruit and vegetables, limes, lemons and oranges, tomatoes, carrots and potatoes, for 100 Ugandan shillings each (about 40p at the official rate of exchange). We are still, literally, 'up-market'.

Descend a mile further down the road almost to the city itself and a nightly candlelit bazaar spreads itself on the shallow sloping ground of a piece of wasteland. Here cheaper foods and clothes are bought and sold by unlicensed traders in what is called the 'Yard Market' for obvious reasons.

In the heart of the city is Nakersero Market with stalls laden with produce and buzzing with activity. Young entrepreneurial pretenders hawk around one-off items for sale: bags, string, magazines and, of all things, wire wool! Judging by the quantities of the latter there is an awful lot of scouring being done in Kampala. Surprisingly perhaps, the erstwhile Asian presence left behind one strange legacy. A few sellers have inherited the trade in eastern spices and are carefully weighing and dispensing small amounts of cumin and curry powder, not normally associated with the African diet.

All very unremarkable one might think except that very little of this would have been taking place just over two years ago. Goods were conspicuous by their absence and Kampala markets and streets for the most part deserted – one piece of evidence of the transformation achieved by President Yoweri Museveni's government. In fact, to the outsider, the bustling signs of activity all over the city – building renovations, new houses, industrial development, tended flower gardens and people scurrying everywhere with bicycles and wheelbarrows – is the most visible indication of a return to normality. But, as everyone admits, there is a long way to go.

Here I find it difficult to get things in perspective. Coloured by the images of twenty years ago and the idealistic commitment one experienced as a young housemaster at Ntare School in Mbarara – the school attended by many of the country's present political and administrative leaders – one cannot avoid a feeling of sadness. The physical destruction since that time has been comprehensive. Roads, schools, hotels and hospitals are unrecognisable.

Even so, meeting former students as I conduct my enquiries has been a rewarding and revealing experience. Like me they have fond memories of Ntare and Will Crichton, the headmaster, now retired back in Aberdeen and overlooking his beloved golf course.[24] The warmth and friendliness I recall are still there. Then, after a few minutes conversation about old times, almost apologetically they look at me and say something like, 'You cannot believe what we have done to this country.' Their bewilderment seems to

---

[24] Will Crichton died several years after retiring from Uganda, and four leading former Ntare students, headed by the First Deputy Prime Minister, attended his funeral service in Aberdeen.

reflect my own thoughts. It's as though earlier 'development', dare one call it progress, was a veneer that peeled away in the sun through sheer neglect and lack of interest. That's not really strong enough, since we know it was more wilful destructive forces than that at work, as the articulate analysis of Professor Samwiri Karugire has made clear in his book, *The Roots of Instability in Uganda*.

Nearly twenty years of tragedy has meant that short-term survival strategies and attitudes have become a way of life and will be difficult to change. As a result, economic irrationalities have been institutionalised. They are particularly prevalent in the public and parastatal sectors. Officially, £1 sterling exchanges for 250 Ugandan shillings but on the free market buys 800. Anyone acquiring foreign exchange at the official rate through trade or overseas travel brings home foreign goods and sells them at local currency prices derived from conversions at the market rate, con-siderably boosting their income in the process. Sales of tea to exporters with barter trade contracts, for example, are handled in this way.

Again, a relatively high-ranking civil servant lectur-ing in the public service college will be paid 2,000 Ugandan shillings a month, barely enough to buy two or three bunches of matoke bananas, the staple food. On a short consultancy assignment he might earn 4,000 shillings an hour! With the cost of living for a reasonable existence in Kampala for someone with a family reckoned to be around 100,000 shillings a month, it is not difficult to see why absenteeism is rife because people are scheming in other directions to acquire enough income to survive. In the circumstances, the level of enthusiasm and industry of some Civil Service officials is remarkable for what amounts almost to voluntary labour. Housing and other allowances offer a partial explanation for their loyalty but the overall rewards cannot compete with the private sector to which many of them have escaped. Hence, the quality of the public service has deteriorated and is a key concern given the extent of the recovery programmes contemplated.

Amidst the sadness there are grounds for optimism. Apart from the obvious signs of recovery and renewal of roads and buildings, the cadre of 1960s' school and university graduates is now occupying senior positions in government, the professions and commerce. Sober, middle-aged men and women with families to protect, in sympathy with the honest attempts of the National Resistance Movement government to erase the degradation of the last two decades are willing to endure austerity and hardship, recognising that it will take some years to shift attitudes and values so long conditioned by fear, cruelty and arbitrary power. A few unconnected incidents, however, suggest that the process has already begun.

A Permanent Secretary, surrounded by desolate, run-down offices, will calmly explain how a certain reform measure has been tabled for Cabinet discussion and once approved will be drafted into a Bill to present to Parliament. Such procedural orthodoxy so soon after anarchical rule by military ruffians is quite amazing.

A government minister is reported in the daily newspaper, the *New Vision*, complaining about being given special treatment by a customs official at the airport who invited him to describe goods acquired during an overseas visit to repair his car as 'personal effects' and thereby exempt from tax. Such a stance must be unique in Africa. Another minister is obliged to resign for brandishing a gun during an argument in a hotel bar.

A couple of National Resistance Army (NRA) soldiers hitched a lift in our car between Entebbe and Kampala. I asked them about the policy of merging the NRA with the remnants of the armies of previous murderous regimes, suggesting that it might cause them some problems. 'Not at all,' one of them replied. 'We shall just tell them, "Why should we fight? We all belong to the same country." We shall politicise them and explain that such hostilities were part of the old politics and are a thing of the past.' Whether they are or not, this boy soldier's account was certainly testimony to the effectiveness of the new leadership's communications.

A series of personal vignettes cannot make an analysis. It merely provides a hazy picture of some aspects of life in and around Kampala.

On one day we drove to Jinja and down to the officially signposted source of the Nile. We stood on the bank opposite the obelisk commemorating Speke.

'Have you been here before?' I asked the driver, Isabirye.

'Yes, once, a long time ago, before you people [the British] left.'

We stared at the flowing river where some desultory planks half-submerged by the water reached out towards a small, rocky island in the Nile some twenty yards from the bank.

'Last time, we walked across there and sat on that rock,' Isabirye said. 'Now it's collapsed.' He paused thoughtfully. 'Since independence, everything's collapsed.' He grinned disarmingly.

I didn't know whether to laugh or cry. Factually, I suppose, he had a point, but the spirit of the people I met – past student friends and newly-made colleagues – will, I sincerely hope, soon prove him wrong.

10

Tea and Sympathy in Bangladesh

A year into the jungle of freelance consultancy and armed with the Mananga approach to management development, I must have been thought suitable material for a stint on the ODA-funded Bangladesh Tea Rehabilitation Project (BTRP) as its Senior Training Adviser. It was an experience which, to the now fully-fledged advocating economist, offered a masterclass in how not to organise a development project.

The plight of Bangladesh has been well rehearsed. Born out of the devastating civil war between East and West Pakistan culminating in its independence in 1971 and largely located on the massive delta formed by the Brahmaputra and Ganges rivers, in the images of the world's media it apparently limps along between disaster-prone floods and dynastic political conflicts. Yet despite being traduced as a 'basket case' country by Henry Kissinger, Bangladesh is rich in resources of rice, tea, fish, natural gas and, above all, in the skills and enterprise of its people whose artistic talents in music, painting, metal crafts and textiles are highly regarded. It has exotically beautiful sunsets magnificently offset by silhouetted sailing boats with the most unusual designs on its many waterways.

The War of Liberation had an enormous impact on the already declining tea industry resulting in low production and yields, repatriation of West Pakistan owners and managers and the destruction of some tea factories. The BTRP was established in 1979 to rehabilitate the tea industry which consisted of 156 tea estates with the majority located around Srimangal and Maulvibazar, and smaller clusters near Sylhet and in the hill tracts near Chittagong.

At Srimangal, management of the project was somewhat oddly located on two sites a mile apart which was not exactly conducive to rapidly assembled team meetings for the allocation of tasks. Of necessity, project vehicles were constantly plying between the two campuses. The old established Bangladesh Tea Research Institute (BTRI), stuffed with scientists to some extent reinventing the wheel since much of the technical side of growing tea was well known and documented, housed the Bangladeshi Project Director who was head of the Project Development Unit (PDU) and several of his staff. A mile up the road was the ODA's wire-fenced enclosure with its main road from the entrance gate snaking past workshops and office blocks and then winding up the hill between staff bungalows culminating in a mini leisure complex with a swimming pool, tennis court, common room and guest accommodation. This is where the bulk of BTRP's combined British and Bangladeshi consultancy team was headquartered. It was also frequented by expatriates escaping from Dhaka braving a bone-shaking drive to reach this little oasis for holiday weekends because it was close to the nearest area of forest and something approaching a hilly landscape in Bangladesh.

The project's locational eccentricity contributed to some of its relationship difficulties. One big happy family it was not! Structural and hierarchical rigidities made things worse. I had an early experience of both. Shortly after arriving I called an informal meeting of the small training team to brief me on the project's training activities. The discussion was barely off the ground before my counterpart, Mr Mahbub, located at BTRI, strongly objected that I had no authority to call a meeting. Only his boss, the Project Director located at the BTRI, could do that. Oh dear! Trivial, I know, but it set the tone for future conflicts.

It also transpired that the expatriate Team Leader to whom I reported had only recently been promoted as joint head of the project from the post I now held as Senior Training Adviser. Mr Mahbub's first allegiance to him, understandably but unhelpfully, persisted throughout my stay. What's more, the Team Leader and I were both engaged by a firm of UK consultants specialising in training. A rival UK firm of traditional tea industry consultants supplied the technical tea experts. This cadre of experienced tea planters had provided earlier Team Leaders of the project prior to the most recent change at the top. Hence a smouldering resentment punctured the atmosphere at their downgrading in the management pecking order, occasionally igniting small explosions at team meetings. To say relationships between the two firms running the tea project, if you'll excuse the pun, were rather strained is something of an understatement.

'Opening a can of worms' and managing a 'hornets' nest' aptly depicted the situation. Fortunately, an impending high-powered ODA mid-term review mission helped to concentrate the mind and focus attention on the BTRP's *raison d'être* rather than its fractured personality disputes.

The preparatory papers for the review mission required some research on my part. The BTRP was ten years old and halfway through its third phase. The main thrust of Bangladesh's tea sector policy was twofold: to generate employment and foreign exchange earnings. Both imply an increase in production of tea. Since there are two ways of achieving such an increase, the twin objectives of the project were to increase yields and expand the area of land under tea. By Phase III it was recognised that the value of output could not only be increased by quantitative measures but could also be enhanced by improvements in quality, which became a third objective. On this latter point, Bangladesh's tea was categorised on the international market along with Malawi's as low to medium grade, or 'filler' tea, suitable for blending with other teas.

By 1989, after ten years, much of the infrastructure development such as repairing factories, replacing equipment, improving roads and providing water supplies was nearing completion. Extension of tea cultivation and replanting of old tea was also well under way. Progress was sufficient to prompt one economic report to conclude that 'the tea industry of Bangladesh is no longer in need of rehabilitation'. It also observed that 'Tea estates are not merely profitable, but highly profitable; several proprietors/groups admit privately that they have not made losses since 1973 despite the screams of industry.'[25]

At this juncture there was definitely a need for a Pinter pause . . . preferably for thought. If things were going so swimmingly what on earth were we all doing in Bangladesh? More importantly, why was British aid still being squandered on a venture that had ostensibly accomplished its development goals? Even more curious, we were being asked to prepare a rationale to present to the review mission for a possible *Phase IV* of the project. It was time to delve a little deeper into the archives.

Let's start with the structure of the tea industry. After partition of the Indian sub-continent in 1947 the area under tea in Bangladesh (then East Pakistan) remained at 30,000 hectares until 1960. A change in government policy led to a rapid increase to 43,000 hectares by the time of independence in 1971. It was only after the start of the BTRP that this was further extended to 47,000 hectares under tea by 1987. This represents less than half the total grant of land to the 156 tea estates of around 112,000 hectares. The remaining non-tea land included 32,000 hectares suitable for extension into tea cultivation, 22,000 occupied by various types of infrastructure such as roads, houses and hospitals as well as labourers' paddy lands, 4,000 under other crops and 6,000 comprising ditches, streams and waste lands.

The ownership of the estates fell into three categories:

---

[25] Shields Report, 1984.

1   *Sterling companies* – registered in the UK, controlled by British management and with shares traded on the London Stock Exchange. They ran 26 of the larger tea gardens on 42 per cent of tea-planted land and produced 50 per cent of the total crop.

2   *Bangladesh companies* – registered in Bangladesh, owning and running one or more estates. The parastatal National Tea Company is included in this group and owned twelve estates. It held 39 per cent of tea-planted land and produced 38 per cent of the total crop.

3   *Bangladesh proprietary estates* – together with the Bangladesh companies, they owned the rest of the 130 estates the preponderance of which were the smaller tea gardens. The proprietary estates held 18 per cent of tea-planted land and produced 12 per cent of the total crop.

Whilst the overall picture in terms of profitability seemed rosy, this disguised the fact that there were many small tea gardens, but not covering a very large area, where productivity was extremely low. Yields were less than 200 kg/hectare compared with an average yield in Bangladesh of around 900 kg/hectare. This, in turn, by international standards was regarded as very modest when neighbouring India was capable of producing about 1,600 kg/hectare. Such marginal estates had great difficulty becoming financially viable and were often referred to as 'sick and derelict' gardens. It may be that a separate agenda was at work here such that the owners of these non-performing gardens acquired them as a means of escaping the national land reform policy of restricting individual land ownership to a maximum of 20 hectares.

So much for the broad economic structure of the project. Now for the really dicey question which must be posed by any expatriate consultant worth his salt struggling to make sense of a long-running development project. Who are the beneficiaries of the project's past and potential benefits?

From the documentary evidence revealed so far about the general and continuing profitability of the tea industry, the first category of beneficiaries was the estate owners, many of whom, for the organised sector, were shareholders resident outside Bangladesh. Others were Bangladeshi shareholders, proprietary garden owners and the government of Bangaladesh from its equity share in the National Tea Company and as the recipient of taxation. Another category of beneficiaries included those families of tea workers that were now better housed as a result of the project and those enjoying potable water supplies and improved sanitation. Trainees that had attended management, artisan and overseas courses constituted a third category.

Thus, in contrast to the ODA's declared policy priority of directing aid flows so that they benefit the 'poorest of the poor' it was likely that the net effect of the project meant a higher take-up of benefits by the organised sector of the industry, whether profit-receiving shareholders or wage-earning communities of workers, rather than the less developed sector of underdeveloped gardens and other lands, together with their populations, in the tea-growing regions.

A chink of light was beginning to shine on the way forward for justifying a Phase IV extension of the project which might keep our paymasters happy. It ran along the lines that in Phase IV there would be a concerted effort to meet this possible objection head on by redirecting the thrust of the project away from concessional financial arrangements for infrastructure investment to the advantage of creditworthy companies and proprietors and towards human resource development throughout all levels of the industry. In this way tangible benefits such as the acquisition of skills through training, better health and conditions at home and work and the generation of new social development and income-earning activities would accrue directly to a large number of Bangladeshis.

Furthermore, a second element in the Phase IV strategy was to address more forcefully the 'less developed garden' (LDG) problem and the general issue of unutilised land in the tea areas with a view to exploring alternative agricultural patterns and introducing more productive activities to the benefit of their resident populations. At one time the fifty or so non-viable, underperforming gardens might *de facto* have been excluded from the project because it was not possible to reach them with the instrumental aid inputs devised for the tea industry. Now it was conceivable that the point might soon be reached where the rehabilitation of the organised sector of the tea industry was deemed to have been completed and hence excluded from the next phase of the project, designed solely to implement integrated rural development initiatives in the LDGs.

As the author of this bit of the confidential

addendum for the ODA mid-term review submission, I was now advocating one-handedly at full throttle. Skating over the notion that some British aid might actually have been lining the pockets of British shareholders, I claimed that the economic justification for a Phase IV was less to do with enhancing the productivity and hence the profitability of a largely private sector tea industry and more about promoting development amongst rural populations in the tea area and its peripheries. This might be achieved via a range of activities designed to raise their income levels and, in consequence, their general living standards and well-being, only one of which might be employment in the tea industry.

I then went on to commit the cardinal sin for a consultant *in situ* on a project. I recommended the phasing out of my own post at the end of Phase III. Sure, there would still be an ongoing need for management development and training throughout the tea industry but there were plans to institutionalise the embryonic Management Training Centre at Srimangal, there were other management training courses available at existing institutes elsewhere in Bangladesh, and the British Council had bursary schemes available to support senior staff training at various colleges in the UK. I argued that my rather costly post could be rationalised out of existence apart from intermittent 'advisory and monitoring' short visits. Big mistake!

From my perspective, the development consultant acts as a catalyst sparking off agreed initiatives, facilitating their resourcing, helping to ensure their sustainability locally and then moving on. Projects were not meant to be permanent features on the landscape but passing phenomena designed to disappear once their purpose had been accomplished. That's not how consultancy firms see them. At worst, there was a desire to perpetuate their activities and also a strong motivation for doing so. Firms pay £x,000 to a consultant on an overseas assignment but charge perhaps £4x,000 as the project cost of keeping them there. Admittedly they've got substantial overheads to meet in the UK and housing, transport, taxation and allowances to cover when the consultant is at the duty station but the mathematics leave a generous margin for profit. Equally there's a substantial loss when any post evaporates.

One day at the office in Srimangal, when our firm's UK Project Director was on one of his monitoring visits, the Team Leader invited me to take a ride in his Land Rover. He wanted a conversation where there was no chance of being overheard. The gist of what he said was that my recommendation, which had been relayed to the UK office, not to put too fine a point on it, had not been warmly received. Rather, it had led to a minor volcanic eruption such that the Project Director, in an apoplectic fit, had just informed the Team Leader that he wanted me off the project as soon as possible and had already begun a shortlist of candidates to replace me. At this point in the proceedings, rather like the man in my namesake, Gerard Hoffnung's, famous 'bricklayer's story' at the Oxford Union, 'I nearly lost my presence of mind'. Instead, I demurred and told the Team Leader that I had signed a contract for a year and, with another six months to run, I intended to fulfil it. There was no way I would accept the offered poisoned chalice to leave the project halfway through. The Team Leader backed me and I didn't, but it was a close call.

Tea is a beautiful crop usually grown in stunning surroundings and best seen from a short distance. Close up, it is thorny and plucking the leaves is painful on the hands. The object of the exercise for securing the best quality tea is to pick the 'two leaves and a bud' on the end of each branch of the bush. As was earlier mentioned, Bangladesh produces tea of poor to medium quality and yet when visiting a tea estate manager on project business and invited to sample the garden's tea it didn't seem that way. Sitting on the verandah of the manager's bungalow within a picturesque landscape overlooking neat rows of tea bushes, the hot bright-orange coloured liquid served in a transparent glass cup and saucer, to which it would be sacrilege to add milk, paradoxically tasted like nectar.

There were many such pleasurable moments in Bangladesh. Opportunities for social interaction were plentiful and I met many wonderful people who lent a sympathetic ear to my problems, as I tried to do to theirs.

In my immediate circle were my bearer, Hannan, and my driver, Modhu. Nearly 200 years of the British in the Indian sub-continent had clearly left its mark. Both of them made my comfort and welfare their prime concern. This seemed a little strange so long after independence, especially to an English person unaccustomed to having servants and with a tendency towards liberal and egalitarian views. But I had learned something from mistakes made in Africa. Somewhere along the way I had been struck by the

133

radical views of an American employer who paid his staff what they asked for and never had any problems with industrial relations concerned with pay. In a small way, I tried it out with Hannan and Modhu who were my personal employees. At first they were baffled and wanted me to tell them what their wages would be. But I held out for a few days until they had thought about it and told me what they wished to be paid. I might add that this was against the advice of one or two established colleagues who were anxious that I should not pay them 'over the odds'. In the event what they requested was in line with that of other staff and our working relationship was very harmonious throughout my stay.

Hannan had honed the practice of service to a fine art. He shopped for food in the market at Srimangal and produced excellent meals. When I wandered into the kitchen for the odd utensil, he would observe me closely and conclude correctly that I was after a teaspoon and even open the drawer to give me one. He was a quiet, dignified man. Modhu was more macho, a big extrovert man full of good humour and a brilliant enterprising driver. I well remember one particular occasion when we arrived at the ferry point en route for Dhaka only to find that the queue of vehicles waiting to board was over a mile long. It would take several ferries and about ten hours waiting time before we would get across. After pausing in the queue for only a few minutes, without saying a word, Modhu moved the Land Rover out of the line, drove almost to the front of the queue and nosed our vehicle in on a level with the fourth car. He then had a loud gesticulating argument with other drivers of which I understood not a word. What on earth he said to persuade them to let him in I cannot imagine but we were on board in no time, much to my relief. It was with great sadness shortly after I returned to England that I received a letter informing me of Modhu's death following a short illness.

Life on the estates could be tricky. History had bequeathed to Muslims the responsibilities of management and to Hindus the supply of their labour. Tensions and tempers sometimes ran high, complicated by religious overtones. Riots between the two religious groups flared up in Srimangal at one point but did not develop. Part of my job involved co-ordinating the selection procedures for sending a party of tea managers for a tailor-made management training course in the UK under the auspices of British Council sponsorship. I visited all the candidates to discuss their training needs during this process. One young manager explained his predicament. He had great difficulty dealing with his labour force, so much so that he felt isolated in his bungalow at night, a frightened man, and at times stones had been thrown onto his verandah.

I next met him a few months after his course on a follow-up visit and discovered a new man. His training had exposed him to a review over several weeks of his managerial duties, problems and actions in the company of a small group of his peers from which he gained new insights into ways he might handle situations differently. The training programme was led by former MAMC staff and provided a similar type of 'Mananga Experience' to that outlined in Chapter 8. This man was living proof of the effectiveness of a good management development programme in changing behaviour and enhancing a manager's confidence to deal with day-to-day problems on the job.

On his return to Bangladesh I found him enthusiastic about his job and no longer demoralised. He now had friendly relationships with his staff and team of labourers and had learned how to communicate with them and take an interest in them. His demeanour was completely transformed. There were other such stories but his was the most dramatic.

As for the project itself, two thirds of the way through my one-year contract the manner of working was increasingly frustrating. I said as much in one of my regular informal letters to the UK office when I wrote that I was coming around to the view that some of our operational difficulties stemmed from the dual administrative/management structure of the project. No matter how good the liaison, inevitably there were two centres of power – the PDU under the Director and the consultancy team under the Team Leader. Even minor matters such as changing the use of a room at the ODA complex had first to be put in the form of a proposal from the consultants to the Director. The PDU then commented on, amended or rejected the proposal as they saw fit. Usually it was the latter. More important initiatives such as co-operating with other projects on their training requirements or developing non-tea activities on unutilised estate land were buried in this bureaucratic quagmire.

This was not how we should be working. I advocated a single administrative structure with a Project Management Committee comprising elements of both groups to speed up decision-making and cut through the needless red tape of duplicated dialogue and endless copied correspondence flowing between the two separate camps when they should be functioning as an integrated unit.

Nothing much changed in the final third of my stay and so the BTRP remained a sobering experience but I wouldn't have missed it for the world. It brought me into contact with a new part of the globe, one teeming with humanity, much of it stoically preoccupied with the business of survival in the face of potentially devastating floods, famines and ferry disasters.

How could one ever forget the sights and sounds of Bangladesh: the women and children astride pyramids of stones, hammering them into rubble to be used as hardcore for roads; the shouting matches between the rickshaw pedallers competing for custom on the chaotic carriageways of Dhaka; the generosity of the lowly paid in giving their loose change to the pleading beggars crowding each transport terminus; the abject poverty of families forced to live in hovels on the city's pavements; the kaleidoscope of colours streaming across watery skyscapes and illuminating the magnetic appeal of the evening bazaars; the privilege of being invited to share *Iftar*, the fast-breaking sunset supper with Bangladeshi colleagues during Ramadan. Years later, the memories of such scenes came flooding back and helped me to appreciate more fully the context of Monica Ali's brilliant novel, *Brick Lane*.

11

Laptop Dancing

Sitting with my longstanding friend, Stephen Brazier, on the verandah of a Kampala restaurant in the heady days of the rebuilding of Uganda in 1993, seven years into its reconstruction and development programme, we observed that to be an international consultant it was essential to be equipped with a laptop computer. It also helped if the owner sported a beard. The place was teeming with such types, usually behind the wheel of a large 4 x 4 vehicle bearing the insignia on its side of the project and sponsor to whom the driver was attached. We were witnessing the high noon of the itinerant expatriate expert.

Everyone in development circles has heard the one about the World Bank consultant who said, 'If it's Tuesday it must be Lesotho.' The worst example of this species I came across was on a visit to Murchison Falls Game Park in northern Uganda. He was a North American journalist staying for the weekend at Paraa Lodge from which vantage point he was about to return home and write an in-depth article full of insights into the country's problems he had gleaned

139

from this brief sojourn, to be syndicated in news-papers across the United States. One could only sit open-mouthed and goggle-eyed listening to this dis-play of ambition and ignorance descending in equal globules of arrogance.

What was it T.E. Lawrence had written in his book *The Seven Pillars of Wisdom*? After riding across deserts on camels with his Bedouin compatriots, adopting their dress and customs, living and sleeping alongside them, he wrote something to the effect that he didn't think he would ever understand the Arabs. If anyone had penetrated another culture he had, and yet he belaboured his lack of knowledge. A phoneti-cally sounding English idiomatic joke doing the rounds in the 1960s defined an expert as follows: 'X' is the unknown factor and 'spurt' is a drip under pressure. Think about it!

I remember at that time a colourful Ugandan Marxist, Makerere University College extra-mural tutor, called Chango Macho, gently chiding his audi-ence at a meeting in Mbarara about British experts coming to Uganda, which they were then doing in droves. 'If a dustman comes to Uganda from Britain he's an expert,' he said. Some embarrassed expatri-ates giggled sheepishly at this frontal assault. He was rightly attacking the idea that anyone from outside should automatically be considered more competent than a Ugandan. Who am I to smirk – wasn't I now guilty of the same thing in my relatively new guise as a freelance consultant? Probably, but clutching at straws I recalled that Winston Churchill once said that we were all worms but he liked to think he was a glow-worm. In a similar vein, several hundred times removed, I clung on to the notion that in all the fun and frustration surrounding overseas development work, it was empathy that mattered and one could only strive to do one's best for the people each project was intended to benefit.

Armed with this wafer-thin rationalisation, I waltzed my laptop around a few more countries, preferably where I was unknown, dropping a few pearls of wisdom acquired from others along the way and never shrinking to offer them as my own.

Short-term consultancy is a curious business. In general, an assignment crystallises from an investigatory mission sponsored by an international agency such as the EU, World Bank, FAO or a national aid authority such as UK's ODA, now DfID. Terms of reference are prepared on the basis of the mission's proposals and another group of people recruited to implement the project that has now emerged from these deliberations, chief of which is the project manager or Team Leader. The more discerning among you will have immediately spotted a fatal flaw in this sequence: the poor souls charged with erecting the project edifice had nothing to do with its design. No wonder there is such mayhem in the start-up phase of many projects.

Having secured a role on a consultancy team, an amazing thing happens. Just before your flight you are deluged with papers and reports from the sponsoring agency indicating that just about everyone in the development community over the last fifty years has visited, comprehensively researched and written about the problem which you thought uniquely yours to solve. With such a wealth of material available already you might be thinking, what on earth is there left to do? When digging around the documents in the Jizan office in Saudi Arabia one day, for instance, I even discovered a report by no less a figure than the notorious Cambridge spy, Kim Philby, spelling out necessary irrigation improvements to boost agriculture in the Wadi Jizan area decades before the project on which I made a brief appearance early in 1972.

Alan Johnson, a very experienced former ODA adviser with whom I worked on an assignment in South Africa, had the best approach of any Team Leader I came across for dealing with voluminous existing records. I met him in the lounge of our hotel where he was seated at a table piled high with paperwork. He explained his prioritising technique to me. Plucking a fattish report off the pile he said, 'This is a three beer report' – meaning he would fillet the bones of it in the time it took to sink three cans of Castle lager. You get the drift. By the time he reached the one-beer category of reports there was not much point in dwelling on them too long. This has a serious side to it, of course, in that the sheer weight of accumulated dossiers, if they were studied too intensively, could mean that they absorbed half the mission time for the new assignment.

African quickstep

Oh well, if it's Monday it must be Malawi! This long, straggling, lakeside country down the spine of central Africa witnessed several of my short sorties into

consultancy land. One of these was for the United
Nations Development Programme to establish whether Malawi's national training institutions (NTIs) had
the capacity to ... wait for it ... take a deep breath ...
support decentralised participatory rural development (DPRD). Phew!

This piece of jargon, roughly translated, meant that
there was a two-pronged strategy for realising the
government of Malawi's Poverty Alleviation Programme. Firstly, there was the nightmare policy area
of decentralisation which sought to clarify the roles
and responsibilities of the key players engaging in
rural development. Essentially this meant removing
the fog covering the overlapping memberships and
activities of three bodies: the local administrative
wings of government ministries; the district development committees; and the local authorities, chiefly
the district councils. There was a growing consensus
towards a single, unified, democratically elected body
taking over all local development work and centred
on the district council. Since this would involve a
massive transfer of power and resources from the
centre to the periphery and a virtual overhaul of the
complete system of government, it remained a con-
tentious issue in the mid-1990s.

Secondly, there was the strategy of participatory
rural development which was striving to get away
from an era of failed attempts whereby rural communities are the supposed beneficiaries of received
wisdom from the apex of power and are systematically left out of decision-making processes which
affect their lives. Decades of following this kind of
top-down, hierarchical approach in Malawi had done

little to alleviate poverty. Instead, it had met with resistance and passive resignation leading to a stifling of creativity and resourcefulness and an expectation of handouts.

The fall-guys in this outmoded structure were the extension agents. Instead of being encouraged and resourced to work innovatively with farmers, utilising existing knowledge and expertise and responding to their needs, problems and suggestions, they were used as messengers charged with conveying information from their ministry overlords telling farmers what they should be doing differently. As a result, extension agents were caught in the crossfire of criticisms from frustrated farmers to whom they had nothing to offer and sour supervisors whose change imperatives could not be implemented. The extension agents had no incentives or freedom of action to break out of this syndrome.

Hence the search for alternative ways of working with poor people to improve their conditions. This is where our assignment came in, which was to investigate how far the NTIs could contribute to that search on the huge assumption that decentralisation would be introduced as an essential backcloth.

Nine NTIs, pretty well all of them, were visited in as many days by my colleague and I criss-crossing the country. As well as the data gathered from discussions with staff and course members from this rapid survey, the report's Executive Summary judiciously records that 'the consultants also took cognisance of the work already done in this area and reported by other missions. Particular note was taken of the key policy documents as the basis for discussions on the context of this inquiry'. This is the standard genuflection towards the work of forerunners. In pursuance of the Alan Johnson dictum, the preliminary beers and papers were not consumed for nothing.

Two institutional visits stand out in my mind. One was to the Forestry Training College situated in the hilly area to the north of the town of Dedza about forty miles south-east of the capital, Lilongwe. The college campus was on the outskirts of a large pine forest which the staff had to manage in addition to their training duties. Ostensibly this was a well-run college with a small well-qualified staff of six tutors and a principal (about the right establishment for its current workload), offering two courses in forestry – a two-year certificate programme leading to appointment as a government forestry assistant and an eighteen-month upgrading diploma programme after at least three years as a forestry assistant leading to promotion to forestry officer grade.

We met an enlightened staff already to some extent employing participatory techniques in their training methodology with ample scope for using the adjacent forestry estate in practical assignments demonstrating wood utilisation and processing, and designing and constructing forest roads and telephone links through the forest, for example, or conducting forestry research. Clearly there was a lot of potential for further development. The downside, it transpired, was that this potential had remained unrealised since the college's foundation in the late 1950s. Nearly forty years on, it quickly became apparent why. In a clichéd phrase, it was largely due to the dead hand of bureaucracy. The college had a splendid site but many of the physical facilities were in dire need of maintenance, a situation which had arisen partly as a result of the centralised financial control system. Fifty motor bikes were available for travelling around the forest, not one of which was on the road at the time of our visit. Of the seven other vehicles, only two were in running order. We learned that minor repairs to motor vehicles and other equipment could not be undertaken locally but had to be referred to headquarters in Lilongwe. Even the purchase of a replacement cup and saucer had to be authorised by the parent ministry and requisitioned from official suppliers. This was a case of bureaucracy run riot and an absurd way to manage a college training adults.

Of course we recognised that the college was constrained by a financial straightjacket which only offered it a fifth of the budget required to manage its functions comfortably. The evidence was all around in the form of non-running vehicles, deteriorating structures, low student intakes and a general feeling of helplessness to do anything about it. Paradoxically there was a new, empty, seventy-five bed hostel so there was spare capacity for new work if only an increase in the staff establishment could be achieved. Sadly, as with other government institutions, there was no incentive for staff to try and overcome some of the severe constraints for themselves. Hence the college was confined to a day-to-day survival strategy.

The other institution I particularly remember investigating was even more extreme. The lakeside Mpwepwe College of Fisheries was founded in 1965. At the time of our visit in 1996 it was in the throes of transition. Extensive building works were in progress

146

constructing new teaching facilities and demolishing or renovating old ones, as part of a World Bank-funded project to establish the college as a regional training and resources centre serving the fishing industries throughout the SADC countries.

It offered pre-service two-year residential courses and in-service one-year upgrading diploma pro-grammes for fisheries officers. The effective training faculty, unusually, was at its establishment level of eighteen tutors but the upheaval due to the building project meant only eighteen students were on course. It was therefore massively overstaffed and even after the expansion its accommodation capacity would constrain student numbers such that it would still have twice as many staff as it needed. The consultants were forced to conclude, somewhat tongue in cheek, that there was excess capacity (staff) for current training needs and too little capacity (accommoda-tion) for future expansion in line with the size of the new infrastructure developments. How could the problem be resolved?

This was pure grist to the mill of the now free-wheeling one-handed economist. Eureka! Quick as a flash it was obvious that the solution to the dilemma must lie in allocating surplus staff resources to new off-campus or non-training projects. Here I must confess to not knowing an awful lot about fishing. The first and last time I sat beside a lake with a bamboo stick for a rod was as a schoolboy at the Serpentine in London's Hyde Park when, despite the odds, I managed to hook a roach. I'm not even partial to eating fish. So what! Here was a golden opportunity to test the much vaunted claim for the power to be derived from the synergy of the group. After all, we were surrounded by expert fisheries officers. We gathered a bunch of them languishing with nothing much else to do and sat sheltered from the sun on the bank of Lake Malawi. Within minutes a rapid audit of staff skills revealed that not only did they know about fish, they were used to messing about in boats on the lake, some had studied business and communications relevant to a range of organisations and all had experience of local markets and dealing with nearby village fishing communities.

As with other NTIs they had a litany of financial and equipment constraints but, like the Forestry College, what really stymied progress was centralised ministerial control and a lack of institutional autonomy – the recurring theme of our mission. In consequence, morale was low and this was emphasised especially at Mpwepwe where the staff were thoroughly bored and frustrated with their level of inactivity. Nevertheless, given the chance to express their ideas for income-generating activities which could provide both resources to the college and incentives to staff, their ingenuity and enthusiasm shone through and it took about ten minutes to come up with the following list.

- Selling fish from the college's fish farm instead of eating it in the dining room.
- Undertaking commercial fishing with the boats and equipment they had, both as an educational training exercise and also a source of profit.
- Running fee-paying courses for Malawi Development Corporation's fishery employees, of which there were several hundred.

- Exploiting their strengths in marine engineering and boat building commercially.
- Offering vocational short courses as an outreach programme. There were around 40,000 people employed in Malawi's fishing industry which constituted a large potential market.

Our little test worked pretty well and offered empirical evidence in support of group synergy. After that heartwarming encounter my laptop was dancing away that evening trying to convert the experience into the persuasive language of formal recommendations.

Limbo dancing in Lilongwe

I find the subject of eugenics anathema. 'The science of improving the human population by controlled breeding for desirable inherited characteristics', as the dictionary defines it holds no appeal for me. Yet by some strange quirk of fate I found myself working in Malawi for an offshoot of the organisation founded by one of the most famous eugenicists of her time, Marie Stopes (1880–1958). She was a Life Fellow of the Eugenics Society and founder of the Society for Constructive Birth Control and Racial Progress. She also founded the first birth control clinic in England in 1920 under the similar title, Mothers' Clinic for Constructive Birth Control. In her writings she makes clear that the purpose of birth control clinics is to 'curtail the breeding of the C3 population' about which she petitioned MPs. She called for the

149

'sterilisation of those totally unfit for parenthood to be made an immediate possibility, indeed made compulsory' and also advocated compulsory sterilisation of revolutionaries, half-castes, the insane and the feeble-minded.

Oddly enough, her first marriage was not consummated and subsequently annulled. A son by her second marriage, Harry Stopes Roe, was apparently cut out of her will because he married a woman who wore glasses and this was bad heredity. She was, to say the least, somewhat eccentric in her views. Fortunately there was no sign of racist overtones when I linked forces with the contemporary organisation bearing her name. The consultancy wing spawned by Marie Stopes International Ltd specialised in providing technical assistance in reproductive health. Amazingly, I was approached to lead a team of six consultants on an ODA-sponsored assignment to draft a Project Memorandum designing a Safe Motherhood Project for Malawi. The amazement soon fell away once I learned that the specialist in this field was only available for one of the four weeks of fieldwork allocated to the task. Hence my promotion.

At the outset this was serious stuff and I was on a steeply inclined learning curve. I quickly discovered that the maternal mortality ratio (MMR) for Malawi, estimated at 620 maternal deaths per 100,000 live births, was among the worst in the world. This resulted from a high fertility rate leading to women having a large number of pregnancies coupled with a high risk of death from the poor quality of health services available to pregnant women. Moreover, the risk of a complication during pregnancy left many women with chronic ill health, reducing the quality of their lives and constraining their ability to work and care for their families. High morbidity levels, given that women constituted 70 per cent of full-time farmers in Malawi and headed 25 per cent of households, had a significant economic impact in terms of reduced agricultural productivity.

For some reason a quotation from one of Scott Fitzgerald's novels, *Tender is the Night*, springs to mind. A character called McKisco is about to fight an absurd duel. Fitzgerald writes, 'Actually he was one of those for whom the sensual world does not exist, and faced with a concrete fact he brought to it a vast surprise.' Here in Malawi we were faced with two deadly, concrete facts and were grappling with the problem of how to deal with them. Conceptually, the goal of the project was straightforward. It was to improve the quality of obstetric care received by women to reduce the twin ratios of maternal mortality and morbidity.

In standard fashion, as with any project investigation, we began by doing a lot of listening and talking to people who already had considerable knowledge of the issues involved. We also had the advantage that two members of the team were Malawians with senior responsibilities in the health service, one heading the Department of Obstetrics and Gynaecology at the College of Medicine in Blantyre and the other in charge of training nurse-midwives at Kamuzu College of Nursing in Lilongwe. After these discussions we carried our enquiries to all three regions with members of the team, visiting in particular health facilities in Dowa, Chiradzulu and Mzimba and many others in

151

and around Lilongwe. The picture gained from this fieldwork confirmed the view of the World Heath Organisation (WHO) that most maternal deaths occur due to medical conditions which have long been preventable or treatable such as puerperal sepsis, post-abortal sepsis, serious wound infection, obstructed labour and haemorrhage.

Essentially, maternal mortality and morbidity would be reduced by actions to bring down the incidence of these complications and improve their management. Hence the mission sought to devise a project where practical and realistic interventions might alleviate the situation at three levels – village, health centre and district hospital – by dealing with three broad problem areas, namely, resource shortages, skill deficiencies and transfer and referral inadequacies.

Under these heads we recommended infrastructure improvements at health centres but only minor works at district hospitals along with the provision of standard packages of maternity equipment and the supply of drugs. Training was a large part of the project, covering pre-service and in-service training for clinical staff and safe motherhood skills for health surveillance assistants and traditional birth attendants. Protocols would also be revised at both national and district levels. Transfer and referral would be addressed by improved transport and communication systems.

At this point I can offer some personal, anecdotal evidence of some of the system's weaknesses when involved with a minor health emergency. At the farthest point reached on a day's safari to Dowa, we were sitting in a village house having useful talks with some traditional birth attendants when my queasy feeling of the morning developed into something worse. After a close acquaintance with a nearby pit latrine it was decided to abort the trip and get me back as quickly as possible to a hospital in Lilongwe. My nausea and temperature increased a few notches during the journey and I was eventually installed, through the good offices of one of my Malawian doctor colleagues, in the Kamuzu Central Hospital. It was not an ideal way to spend my first weekend of the mission but I was lucky enough to be allocated a bed in the Presidential Suite of the Intensive Care Unit. Despite the fact that these were, presumably, the best health facilities Malawi had to offer, I was not greatly encouraged by the remark of one expatriate doctor who said, 'If you want to get better, you should get out of here as soon as possible.'

During my two-night stay I was treated for possible cerebral malaria, a most unlikely diagnosis since I had barely been in the country for a week. My right arm was wired up to various drips and at night I became quite adept at catching mosquitoes with my left hand as they fluttered in through the un-netted open window. I gleaned a lot about the difficulties of communication in this short sojourn. Whilst I was well cared for by the staff, I was also in splendid isolation. They were stationed about a hundred yards away near to the main group of ward patients. Consequently, if I wanted a nurse for anything I had to shout at the top of my voice to try and attract her attention.

When I got out, I visited the British High Commission's doctor who had a look of resignation on his face when I told him I was staying at the Capital Hotel. It seemed that I was most likely to have had a dose of viral dysentery like the succession of other hotel guests trooping into his surgery. Back at the hotel, I discovered from the smiling steward who looked after my room that the bottled water carefully placed on the bedside table had not been equally carefully boiled and refrigerated but had been filled from the tap in the bath.

At least my suffering had not been in vain and I had learned at first hand some of the problems pregnant mothers must face when complications arise. Other obvious deficiencies confronted them in an emergency. How would a woman in a remote area get to a health centre? Who would take the decision? How would the cost be covered? If they managed to get to a health centre or district hospital would they receive treatment? One of the most awful aspects was to hear that qualified staff would not treat a sick patient because there were no surgical gloves and they feared contracting AIDS.

Somewhat unbelievably, future development in the training of nurses prioritised masters degree programmes for graduate nurses. This would ensure that even more trained personnel would remain near the 'bright lights' in the big towns when there was an urgent need for more staff with basic skills ready to serve their home communities in outlying districts.

What does limbo dancing have to do with all this? Without wishing to stretch a metaphor out of existence, such a dance requires the performer to gyrate to rhythmic music while bending backwards to squeeze himself under a continuously lowered bar resting between uprights. If it's not too far-fetched, the height of the bar may be thought of as a budget constraint and the project task was to get the biggest

154

possible dancer successfully under it. Just another way of looking at the idea of maximising an objective subject to certain constraints – for the mathematically inclined – linear programming by another name.

In the end, our deliberations put forward to ODA and the government of Malawi a £4.1 million project proposal for their consideration. It elaborated interventions in the three broad problem areas already alluded to in the form of detailed activities for improving district maternity facilities in respect of infrastructure, equipment, transport, communications, staff training and management protocols.

The projected outcomes after five years included the establishment of 'safe motherhood plans' in eight districts incorporating the renovation and re-equipment of four district hospitals and over 100 health centres; improved transport and referrals by the provision of ambulances and motor cycles; and enhanced communications with the supply of solar radios. Short courses of appropriate training would also be offered to around 1,200 medical personnel at all levels in the health care system in the eight selected districts along with the development of national and district safe motherhood protocols.

If the changes advocated were accomplished, the consequent improvement in the quality of obstetric services would reduce all-cause maternal mortality and morbidity by an estimated 64 per cent by the final project year. Within the target population of 2.1 million people, this translated into nearly 1,000 deaths and around 6,000 serious complications of pregnancy being averted. Not a bad return for an expenditure of 39p per capita per year.

Consultants' reports may often be left to gather dust on the shelf of some Ministry office and never see the light of day. In this case, although the gestation period was over two years, I know that something happened in the wake of our findings because I saw DfID's recruitment advertisement for project staff in *The Economist*. That filled me with a nice glow for a day or two.

Last tango in Pretoria

On to South Africa – it must be Sunday! No prizes for guessing that 'last tango' refers to the prolonged dance of death of the Afrikaner Nationalist Party government before it faded from political power in 1994. Two years before the African National Congress (ANC) came into their own as the new government of South Africa, one couldn't quite imagine that Nelson Mandela would occupy the huge Union Buildings in Pretoria as the country's first black President.

The excitement in anticipation of a momentous political change was almost tangible. It infected the deliberations of our eleven-member, international, multi-ethnic Review Team. The 'outsiders' included Alan Johnson and myself, engaged by the ODA, and two GTZ consultants from Germany. The rest were 'insiders' from various organisations in South Africa save for one Irishman working as an education consultant in Lesotho. The review in question covered technical and vocational education and training (TVET) in South Africa. Its report endeavoured to reduce the complexities of the existing system, still administered by fifteen separate Ministries of Education in the dying years of apartheid, and provide an outline vision of a unified TVET sector.

This is not the place to write a précis of a lengthy report but rather to indicate the scope and methodology of the review which, for me, worked better and was more rewarding than any other assignment I undertook. Early discussions identified three main streams of provision in the TVET sector – the technikons, the technical colleges and a number of institutions/organisations also engaged in formal and informal TVET activities. The consultancy team split into sub-groups to investigate these three sectors, adding a fourth economic component to the work of the review. I could wear my one-handed economist's hat again with a vengeance. After about ten days in a ghastly hotel in Pretoria working on preliminaries and sorting out fieldwork itineraries, the sub-groups set off to traverse South Africa on a series of visits designed to take a snapshot of current TVET provision and its potential capacity for change and development.

On our return to the capital I decided to find a place more conducive to work in than the original hotel. That's when I discovered a two-storey, serviced apartment block untouched by modern developments with parking and a gated entrance through pleasant gardens. It was clean and basic with facilities for modest self-catering and convenient for the project office located in the Commission of the European Community's office and within easy reach of other members who had decided to move to a better hotel on the same side of town.

A few days later, a GTZ colleague decided to take

another apartment in the same block and then two or three of the South Africans commuting occasionally to keep an eye on their other occupational responsibilities shared a third. These accidentally arranged accommodations were crucially significant when drafting the final report. Living in the same building, about half the team could meet at the drop of a hat and could repair to the privacy of their own rooms to pummel out new sections on their laptops.

Platter meals were taken together in breaks from this hive of activity, washed down with superb South African wines, strengthening the bonds of professional relationships into friendships. Towards the final deadline this manner of working became so intensive that writing logjams when we were too exhausted to continue might be broken by someone waking with inspiration in the middle of the night or early in the morning and resolving the dilemma with a creative introductory paragraph here or a succinct concluding sentence there. These messages would then be conveyed to other members of the team on slips of paper passed under the doors of their rooms.

In this way we were able to complete the report 'in country' before the team dispersed and to make a presentation to a large group of invited stakeholders interested in the review's findings. These addressed the overriding theme of the fragmentary nature of the TVET system with a raft of national, sector and sub-sector recommendations. To achieve articulation of the system as a whole there was a need for a national body co-ordinating education and training activities relating to planning and policy formulation, certification, accreditation of qualifications and the widening of access to potential learners outside the system. A series of sector-wide recommendations spotlighted the need to change the culture of the organisational arrangements via staff development programmes and to extend provision to marginalised groups by developing new curricula and access to funding sources. At the sub-sector level were a flood of ideas that emerged from the team's separate fieldwork visits and enquiries for strengthening specific institutions operating in the sector to gear them up in readiness for an expansion of capacity.

The Review Team's findings were set in the context of the lively debate taking place in South Africa as to the policies which should be stressed for improving the performance of the economy. Since the TVET system aimed at enhancing the employability and productive activity in both the formal and informal sectors of society, to that extent it was driven by the needs of economic development. That was the strategic logic of our deliberations.

Here is where I had some fun with the question: 'Whose economic analysis should we follow?' At the time, there appeared to be three main contending views, each implying an array of policies with its own stakeholder supporters. They all agreed that South Africa was experiencing recession bordering on a slump in the early years of the 1990s but differed as to its causes and cures.

In the first scenario, orthodox market economists argued that when an economy is plainly not operating at the full employment level there must be frictions in the system preventing markets from operating freely so that prices distorted, and no longer reflected, the true costs of goods and resources. By this token unemployment is high because the 'price' of labour – real wages – is too high. Companies therefore economise on labour and move into more capital-intensive production techniques. Correspondingly in the capital market, by contrast, the interest rate is too low and does not reflect the real cost of capital. As a result the economy ends up using more of its scarce resource, capital, because it is cheap and less of its abundant resource, labour, because it is expensive.

Economists of this school of thought looked to the newly industrialised countries (NICs) in the Far East for policy prescriptions to remove market distortions, attributing their rapid economic advance to low labour costs, almost free trade and realistic exchange rates. This approach was also associated with an export-orientated growth strategy. It focused on a renewal of the manufacturing sector by expanding the markets for value-added manufactured products derived from minerals currently exported in a semi-raw state. It saw high-value, capital and skill-intensive exports as having greater demand potential on world markets and hence for economic growth in South Africa, than that for 'low cost, low quality' consumer goods on the domestic market, limited as it was by a badly skewed distribution of income.

The real villains for the adherents of this scenario, whose interference caused price distortions, were the government and monopolistic organisations on both sides of industry. Reformists therefore advocated privatisation of economic activities managed by the state and anti-trust laws to curb monopolistic practices by other organisations.

160

In the second economic scenario, critics of main-stream market economics regarded it as ahistorical and essentially flawed since the preconditions for its successful operation were so restrictive that in reality no entirely 'free' market can ever exist. An economy never returns by itself through some self-balancing mechanism to a situation in which all resources are fully employed. Hence, the economy has to be managed, particularly if it is performing at a low level of activity.

They also had a different take on the NICs' success, citing South Korea, for example, as a country which deliberately interfered in financial markets to attract scarce capital into selected industries at negative real interest rates. It was this price 'distortion' engineered by the government that helped industry to invest in new technology and increase productivity, enabling South Korea to compete internationally. Market failure, therefore, was the reason for government to influence the operation of the market in a certain direction. Since the basic feature of a slump was a reduction in aggregate purchasing power for the economy's goods and services, leading to a fall in production and employment, the government's role was to take action to try and expand consumer and investment expenditure. Here was the voice of an unreconstructed Keynesian speaking!

A policy of 'inward industrialisation' was also adopted by this viewpoint. An estimated 60 per cent of South Africa's population was urbanised. Growing urbanisation creates a demand for low-cost consumer products and prompts the growth of small businesses and workshops into production to meet it. Local

161

researchers in South Africa, however, observed that the most likely candidates for inward industrialisation were industries with low capital and skill requirements such as those producing non-electrical machinery, furniture, clothing, leather goods, metal products, footwear, food and transport equipment. Of these that were open to entry by small firms, only the first two had income elasticities substantially greater than 1. In other words, for most of these items, people didn't spend much more on them as their incomes rose. Furthermore, it was argued that large injections of funding would be needed to spark off the process of industrialisation via this route in view of the low level of domestic demand in terms of purchasing power.

The third analytical scenario looked historically at the long-term development of capitalism. It saw that periodic slumps and crises were endemic to the system and that the necessary concomitant of the unfolding of a capitalist economy over time was the development of a functional underclass. Eventually, in the more teleological versions of this approach, the system would exhaust itself and be supplanted by an altogether different production and social model.

Writers in this mould sometimes offer deeper insights into how the technical and social relations of production currently prevailing in a country have come into existence, refined in South Africa's case to allow for the impact of apartheid, and often talk in terms of 'late capitalism'. They are less specific in their policy prescriptions but inclined towards the interventionist model, being prepared to sacrifice some economic growth for the distributional benefits

162

gained in meeting the rising consumption expectations of a wider cross-section of the community.

Much of the foregoing relates to the modern sector of the South African economy including both formal and informal sectors, but it barely touches the two-fifths of the population living in the rural subsistence economy. On the other hand (Whoops!), the peculiarities of the migrant labour system meant that the latter was untypical of subsistence economies elsewhere in Africa.

It had been estimated, for example, that over half the 'homeland' population was effectively urbanised since state efforts to maintain the migrant labour system had undermined their agricultural production. Subsistence farming, therefore, no longer supplemented household incomes remitted by migrants and provided no cushion against unemployment in the towns and cities. Income from agriculture, including subsistence crops, contributed less than 10 per cent of total income for most rural households in the homelands whose inhabitants were increasingly becoming rural consumers rather than rural producers.

The complexity of the rural economy required land reform coupled with an investment programme of carefully constructed community-based development projects as a means of revitalising an ailing agriculture and alleviating rural poverty. As with other economic development strategies, this had implications for the providers of the necessary training in skills needed to implement such programmes.

In a sense the three economic scenarios just outlined spawned three development models, each with its own stakeholder supporters. What might be termed a 'Corporate Model' was derived from the National Training Strategy prepared at the request of the National Training Board. Under this model the TVET system would be driven by the needs of private industry. It envisaged a privatisation of the TVET system controlled by a decentralised network of Accredited Training Boards ultimately governed by the market for the products of private business.

An 'Administrative Model' based on the Department of National Education's Education Renewal Strategy sought to remove recognised deficiencies in the education and training system and offered a package of reforms enabling it to turn out people better equipped for life, and more of them. The best institutions should be preserved and standards raised in the rest. The eventual goal was a streamlined, equitable, education system.

Both these development models and their advocates, the private sector business community and the education establishment respectively, confined the state to a relatively passive role. Neither of them appeared to appreciate that many of the problems then facing South Africa could be interpreted as an extreme case of market failure. The market had failed to create employment for the majority of the population, economic activity had declined and rural and urban poverty had become widespread. A key element contributing to this situation was the differentiated education and training system linked with other restrictive practices, both social and industrial, which effectively stifled the educational development and advancement of large sections of society for several decades.

The policy prescriptions of the Administrative and Corporate Models were hardly likely to unravel the existing inequalities. Decentralised, autonomously governed education and training institutions might well preserve their exclusiveness by rationing access on the basis of price and income. The TVET system was historically so skewed in favour of the privileged white community that unfettered market solutions were untenable.

The situation called for much more drastic intervention, which was presumably why a 'National Recovery Model' was favoured by the African National Congress (ANC) and the Congress of South African Trade Unions (COSATU) as it presented a comprehensive overhaul of the whole system, setting it in its proper context as one of the central components in revitalising the economy towards the goal of full employment. The TVET system was an instrumental variable alongside other measures such as macroeconomic planning, regulated markets and active government designed to lift the economy out of the doldrums.

That, at any rate, was the thrust of the Review Team's final presentation to stakeholders. Not surprisingly, two years from ascending into power, ANC and COSATU representatives in the audience welcomed the emphasis in the recommendations on transformation of the TVET system. By redressing inequalities, widening access and introducing greater mobility through better co-ordination and articulation, it reflected their own policy priorities. The tango was winding down and the break dancing was about to begin.

12

Banking on Disaster

Just as I was sitting down to write this final chapter,
facing the hopeless task of struggling to reconcile the
various strands of my gentle argument that advocacy
governs economic affairs rather than analysis,
expressed in the form of a path-breaking thesis on the
nature and process of development, the financial
globe suddenly tilted on its axis. The tectonic plates of
the world economy shunted sideways. Whatever the
metaphor used to describe it, there was a paradigm
shift the likes of which had not been seen since the
Wall Street Crash of October 1929 which heralded the
Great Depression of the 1930s. One-handed economics came into its own with a vengeance as one
extreme ideological position gave way to its opposite.
The twin peaks of market capitalism and state natio-
nalisation swapped places as the international banking world imploded before our eyes. What came to be
known in the shorthand phrase as the 'credit crunch'
occurred in September 2008 but the fires stoking the
explosion had been lit many years earlier. How did
this seismic eruption occur? What were its ingredients

and what did it portend for the future? Enough for two final chapters rather than just one.

First we need a little on the fundamentals of banking practice from which all else stems. Back in the 1950s when I was a junior clerk in a Lombard Street bank – the Guaranty Trust Company of New York, which in 1959 merged with J.P. Morgan – there were restrictive rules governing the distribution of assets on the balance sheet of a bank. Deposits by customers represent liabilities to a bank which has to keep sufficient cash on hand to meet possible withdrawals. As the banking system developed from its origins with goldsmiths storing money in the form of gold bullion on behalf of clients, it was gradually realised that they never all wanted to take their money out at the same time.

By the middle of the twentieth century the Bank of England, as the central bank of the UK, required banks to maintain a reserve asset ratio of cash to deposits of 8 per cent. For obvious reasons this was known as the Cash Ratio and the cash could either be held 'in hand' at the banks' tills or on their accounts at the Bank of England. To meet unexpectedly heavy demands for withdrawals, banks held other 'liquid' assets in addition to cash in the form of short-term loans known as 'money at call and short notice' which could be recalled within twenty-four hours, and Treasury Bills which are three-month loans to the government. The latter were purchased at a discount for less than their face value, earning a 'discount rate of interest' when they matured and were repaid at their full value by the Bank of England as the government's bank. Holding Treasury Bills in multiples of £5,000, with different maturity dates, had the advantage of providing banks with renewable flows of cash as well as the facility of being able to re-discount them early if they wanted more cash than expected to meet customers' withdrawals, for example, at Christmas time. These liquid assets acted as a further protective cushion which could readily be turned into cash quickly – which is the definition of liquidity. As such, they earned some interest and from the banks' perspective were preferable to cash which earned none. The second basic rule laid down by the Bank of England that banks had to observe, was that their total liquid assets including cash had to be at least 30 per cent of their total deposit liabilities. Hence, unsurprisingly, it was called the Liquidity Ratio.

Banks earned the major part of their profits from longer-term lending comprising the remaining 70 per cent of their balance sheet assets in the form of investments, mostly in government bonds, as well as loans to individual customers and companies on which higher rates of interest were earned.

In essence, banks created money on the basis of new cash deposits entering the system, limited by these two fundamental ratios. To clarify this point: if a bank received a new cash deposit of £100, it would only need to keep £8 as a cash reserve for safety and could make loans of a maximum of £92 to other customers. Assume the latter spend it all on goods and services and that the recipient shopkeepers and suppliers deposit all the £92 in other banks. They play by the same Bank of England rules and in aggregate they would retain 8 per cent or £7.36 for safety as cash and lend the remaining £84.64 to other customers. This process can continue by similar iterative rounds taking the form mathematically of two convergent geometric series – one for cash and one for loans as follows:

Cash: £8 + £7.36 + £6.77 ...

Loans: £92 + £84.64 + £77.86 ...

When there is a cash ratio of 8 per cent in force for the banking system, the formula for calculating this type of geometric progression is $a/1-r$ where a is the first term of the series. In our example, $a = £8$ for the cash series and $a = £92$ for the loans series. For the second round, 92 per cent of the £8 will be retained in the system as cash, i.e. £7.36, and 92 per cent of the £92 lent by the first bank, once it has been spent by its customers and re-deposited by the recipients elsewhere in the banking system, will become available for new loans, i.e. £92 x 0.92 = £84.64. The formula means a is divided by $1-r$ and r is called the common ratio and in this illustration is 0.92 (i.e. 92 per cent expressed as a decimal) – the ratio by which each term in the series is multiplied to obtain the next term.

Hence the total cash retained by banks is: 8/1–0.92 = £100

and the total loans made by banks is: 92/1–0.92 = £1,150

Thus, the total deposit liabilities for the banking

system as a whole amount to £1,250, of which 8 per cent or £100 is in the form of cash and £1,150 is new money created on accounts throughout the banking system.

This simplified account of the mechanism by which banks create credit and money is at the heart of the crisis of 2008, amplified as we shall see by changes in the regulatory regime and constant innovations by the financial services industry creating new and ostensibly sophisticated products. It should be apparent from this outline that any relaxation in the Cash and Liquidity Ratios would mean that banks could expand their holdings of non-liquid assets and gain higher interest returns and hence profits. The seeds of later financial destruction were sown in a series of institutional changes in the second half of the twentieth century designed to do just that – increase the profitability of financial institutions. The changes could also be interpreted as the progressive ideological realisation of a virtually unfettered market in an increasingly dominant financial sector of the economy.

The first big change was introduced in 1971 by the Bank of England under 'Competition and Credit Control', the primary result of which was to remove the relative straitjacket of the Cash and Liquidity Ratios which restricted the commercial banks' ability to make advances and other long-term loans. They were also discriminatory in that they did not apply to merchant banks and foreign banks, which reduced the effectiveness of monetary control, since they could be circumvented by using other unregulated banks. The Cash and Liquidity Ratios were therefore replaced with one Reserve Asset Ratio of 12.5 per cent. Eligible reserve assets kept by banks had to be 12.5 per cent of eligible liabilities which consisted of Sterling deposits and the new ratio now applied to all banks, allowing greater competition in the banking industry.

In 1981 the Bank of England set out its ideas for prudential supervision of banks' liquidity in a paper entitled *The Liquidity of Banks*. These ideas were formalised in the Bank's 1982 policy notice on *The Measurement of Liquidity* in which the concept of a Reserve Asset Ratio was abolished altogether. The policy notice outlined principles which banks should observe in order to be capable of meeting their obligations to repay deposits when required. By this it meant maintaining access to a prudent mix of different forms of liquidity, and not much else. Hence it states that, 'The responsibility for ensuring the liquidity of a bank rests with its own management. The bank does not seek to impose across-the-board liquidity ratio norms ... and thereby to supplant the exercise of judgement by bank managements'. Talk about giving the banks *carte blanche*! One can almost hear the banks' sighs of relief as the chains fell off. The International Monetary Fund (IMF) recorded the UK's voluntary cash reserve ratio in 1998 as 3.1 per cent and still falling.

Next on the scene are the 'Bankers of Basel', not to be confused with the *Gnomes of Zurich* which was the disparaging term used by Prime Minister Harold Wilson in 1965 to describe the Swiss bankers who he claimed were speculating against the pound sterling. Perhaps he had a point since his Labour government was forced to devalue the pound in 1967. Having given up on controlling liquidity, the central bankers of the G10 developed industrial countries, meeting as the Basel Committee on Banking Supervision housed at the Bank of International Settlements, decided in 1988 to switch tack and proposed a capital requirement for the regulation of banks in the 'Basel I Accord' which has subsequently been fleshed out in the 'Basel II Accord' and its many updates. A new *Capital Ratio* was introduced defined as the percentage of a bank's capital to its risk-weighted assets.

The regulatory waters get very murky from here on but start simply with bank capital being divided into two tiers. Tier 1 (core) capital consists of shareholders' equity, meaning the amount paid to originally purchase the stock of the bank, plus retained profits less any accumulated losses. Tier 2 (supplementary) capital covers Revaluation Reserves reflecting, say, the increased valuation of a bank's headquarters property over time; General Provisions for expected future losses; Hybrid Instruments near equity in nature that could sustain face-value losses without triggering a liquidation of the bank; and Subordinated-term Debt not redeemable for a long term and ranked lower than that of ordinary depositors of the bank.

A federal bank's holding company would be regarded as adequately capitalised with a Tier 1 capital ratio of at least 4 per cent, a combined Tier 1 and Tier 2 Capital Ratio of at least 8 per cent and a leverage ratio (Tier 1 capital/risk adjusted average assets) of at least 4 per cent.

At first glance, this looks like a return to the straitjacket restrictions on bank lending of the 1950s. But against that we need to remember that the Basel

Accords were not a set of rules but a guidance framework, which might or might not be adhered to and in any case, was subject to individual interpretation by the national central banks. Paradoxically, repeated attempts to stabilise banking behaviour had the net effect of giving the banks more freedom to increase their profit-making activities by the creative invention of more and more reckless financial instruments circumventing any regulatory obstacles ostensibly barring their way.

The juggernaut of deregulation rolled on across the Atlantic with the arrival of Collateralised Debt Obligations (CDOs) and Credit Default Swaps (CDSs) on the scene, derivatives which were developed towards the end of the twentieth century. As they turned out to be the harbingers of the devastating credit crunch in the autumn of 2008, they merit closer examination.

A CDO is an asset-backed security, the latter being a document held by a creditor guaranteeing a right to payment. The assets can include mortgage-backed securities, corporate loans, credit card loans and even other CDOs. A CDO has been described as like a box full of diced-up assets. Investment banks typically issue CDOs as bonds and use the proceeds to purchase a portfolio of underlying assets. CDOs are issued in different tranches. Senior CDOs are paid from the cash flows from the underlying assets before the junior CDOs and equity securities. Any losses are borne first by the equity securities, next by the junior CDOs and finally by the senior CDOs. Ratings agencies such as Moody's and Standard and Poor were persuaded that the top tranche of 'safe' assets warranted their highest AAA rating, meaning that they were virtually a zero credit risk. With this stamp of approval, even though it did not apply to other more risky elements in the box of assorted assets on which the CDOs rested, they became attractive to banks that could convert their riskier mortgages and other loans into seemingly higher grade paper, prompting a massive expansion in the number of CDOs created. The issuing houses earned commission at the time of issue and management fees during the life of the CDO, and for investors the CDO earned higher rates of return compared with alternatives such as Treasury Bills. The fact that they contained a structural flaw in the form of incentives for the originators of the underlying assets to emphasise the quantity of loans offered, rather than their quality, was either ignored or unnoticed.

The second major derivative innovation, CDSs, entered the scene in 1997 at the hands of the 'J.P. Morgan mafia'. A CDS is an agreement between two counterparties, in which one makes periodic payments to the other in return for a promise of a payoff if a third party defaults. The first party is the 'buyer' and gets credit protection, and the second party is the 'seller' and gives credit protection. The third party with the potential to default is called the 'reference entity'.

In short, a CDS offered insurance cover to anyone holding an investment security underwritten by loans which would leave them exposed to losses if those loans defaulted. Already we can see an obvious connection to candidates that would benefit from this protection racket, namely the massive amounts of CDOs piling up in banks and other finance

175

institutions. Their owners were getting a bit twitchy in case the foundation assets on which their CDOs were based turned sour. Hence they were only too willing to hedge their bets by shifting this risk burden onto someone else's shoulders – namely the sellers of CDS protection. For this privilege they paid insurers such as the firm AIG a regular premium. For example, if Bank A writes a mortgage for a £1 million house to, in that glorious phrase, a 'reference entity' which presumably is a euphemism for a human being, and it's worried the latter might default on its loan repayments, it will buy CDS protection from Bank B and pay a monthly premium for the next five years or whatever is the life of the loan. In return, Bank B agrees to pay Bank A the value of the mortgage if the owner defaults.

Meanwhile, between the late 1990s and 2006, the price of houses soared in the United States, associated in particular with a surge in 'subprime lending' which, according to George Akerlof and Robert Shiller in their book, *Animal Spirits*, quadrupled in size to 20 per cent of the mortgage market at around $625 billion. A prime loan is one backed by good collateral and unlikely to fail to honour its contractual payment obligations in servicing the loan. By contrast, subprime mortgage loans were aggressively marketed among low income, ill-informed, vulnerable people with a high risk of defaulting if market conditions changed. Unlike earlier times when lenders held mortgages until they matured, the originators of subprime mortgages rarely did but instead sold them on to financial institutions which repackaged them into 'sliced and diced pools of mortgages' to quote the economist Paul Krugman's graphic phrase[26] and sold them to investors in the form of CDOs.

The probability of default was small when house prices were rising steeply and the losses expected were low, which is why the rating agencies felt able to give them AAA ratings. Those who bought these junk bonds wanted the higher returns offered and didn't question too closely their AAA rating. The packagers of the bonds would also have gone to rival rating agencies if one of them gave a lower rating. Thus everyone in the supply chain had an interest in not blowing the whistle on the inherent vulnerability of these complex derivatives since they were predicated on house prices continuing to rise in the future as they had been doing in the recent past.

Parallel with these developments there was a significant political intervention which downgraded still further the impact of banking regulation and lubricated the explosive expansion of the CDO and CDS markets. Since the Great Depression of the 1930s, the Glass-Steagall Act of 1933 had separated commercial banks and their key functions of accepting deposits from, and making loans to, individuals and firms, from investment banks which raise money by issuing and selling securities. Commercial banks were also forbidden from getting into the insurance business. These wise legal constraints were irresponsibly overthrown by the passage of two Acts through Congress at the end of the twentieth century.

In 1999, Senator Philip Gramm, a *'laissez-faire*

---

[26] Krugman, P. (2008) *The Return of Depression Economics and the Crisis of 2008*. London: Penguin.

ideologue from Texas' according to one commentator, Matt Taibbi, writing on the economic crisis in 2009, co-sponsored a Bill that repealed the Glass-Steagall Act that had prevented the creation of giant financial conglomerates like Citigroup. It removed the protection offered by smaller banks that knew their local clients personally and their credit worthiness for loans. That mode of doing banking was now disappearing as financial institutions became more remote from their customers and sold on loans at the drop of a hat in complicated parcels of mixed-loan debts, as outlined earlier, in the pursuit of further profits. The Gramm-Leach-Bliley Act of 1999 gave the legislative green light to commercial banks to engage in CDO transactions.

In 2000, the same Senator Gramm wrote a new law called the Commodity Futures Modernization Act which made it impossible to regulate CDSs as either a form of gambling or a security. This Act triggered the growth in the CDS market estimated at around $60 trillion by 2008 and earned the Senator the accolade of 'high priest of deregulation' from the 2008 Nobel Laureate in Economics, Paul Krugman.

These two Acts effectively demolished the distinction between commercial banks and investment banks. The conservative, safe-lending culture of ordinary retail commercial banks became embroiled with the high risk, casino-like gambling for high stakes activities which characterised the behaviour of the investment banks. Both were now competing in the same markets for derivatives which were virtually outside the scope of the regulatory authorities.

We have now identified the four key ingredients

that led to the financial and economic crisis that surfaced in the autumn of 2008, namely, the creation of collateralised debt obligations, the associated insurance protection that emerged as credit default swaps, a crazy bubble in house prices and the culmination of progressive deregulation in the financial sector so that the most virulently expanding financial instruments had no regulation whatsoever. The United States and Britain led the way with these developments but other countries followed suit in financial centres around the world. We can think of them as rather like the Four Horsemen of the Apocalypse galloping headlong towards inevitable catastrophe.

There is a simple empirical fact about rapidly inflating bubbles: after a while they burst. House prices in the United States started sagging in 2006 and plummeted in 2007. Subprime mortgage borrowers faced jacked-up interest rate repayments after the grace period of low interest rate sweeteners had passed which had initially persuaded them that they could afford the loans. In fact they could not afford them. They defaulted and were foreclosed. Thousands of un-resaleable properties came onto the market, often trashed in anger by their outgoing owners.

The shadow banking system, comprising non-regulated financial institutions that had spearheaded the exponential growth of CDOs and CDS insurance protectors, had created a top-heavy inverted pyramid of credit resting on a tiny platform of real assets in the form of subprime mortgages. When the subprime market collapsed, the shadow banking system faced possible meltdown. Bear Stearns, one of the 'big five' major US investment banks, was in difficulties in

179

March 2008. It disappeared off the scene but the Federal Reserve, America's central bank, together with the Treasury, acted to protect its 'counterparties' – those to whom Bear Stearns owed money in financial deals.

The expectation was that the financial authorities would do the same when Lehman Brothers got into trouble but instead they let the firm go to the wall on 15 September 2008, a disastrous move in Paul Krugman's view, which triggered a complete downfall in confidence. Asset prices nosedived and sources of credit dried up to such an extent that banks were unwilling to lend to other banks on the short-term money markets. This was the 'eye of the storm'. Panic was taking over and the giant US insurer AIG was effectively nationalised to try and stem the rot. Borrowers tried to repay their debts by selling assets and banks withdrew credit. Bonds resting on high risk mortgages had been so widely sold that the whole system was infected. As their sales had exploded exponentially so the retreat from them was equally exponential. 'Trillions of dollars in credit disappeared', to quote Paul Krugman yet again. The global financial system was grinding to a halt, dragging down the 'real' economy in its wake. Consumption spending declined as people sought to pay off their debts, unemployment soared and production dropped.

Here was a classic 1930s Depression scenario calling for rescue by the Keynesian cavalry. If the whole economy is in the doldrums and fails to respond when interest rates sink to the floor – for example, the historically unprecedented low level of 0.5 per cent set by the Monetary Policy Committee of the Bank of England – then there is only one actor capable of stopping the slide and boosting aggregate expenditure and that's the government.

Unfortunately, Keynesian remedies had been in the wilderness for so long that nearly everyone with any clout as an economic adviser or policy-maker was a Friedmanite monetarist and dyed in the wool market system ideologue. In the phrase used by Michael Sandel in his 2009 Reith Lectures, we had experienced three decades of 'market triumphalism' with its arrogant belief that markets would always find a rational, efficient solution to all economic problems. It took a while for the authorities to realise that the whole edifice of that creed had tumbled to the ground.

Governments and their monetary authorities peered over the brink into the abyss of a breakdown in the global financial system and scrabbled to salvage something from the wreckage. Enter the ghost of John Maynard Keynes. From Wall Street to Lombard Street and other international financial centres, the word on the lips of members of the central banks, regulators and Treasury ministers was 'bailout'. The banks would be bailed out with gargantuan injections of cash with the objective of removing the paralysis in the credit system. Furthermore, aggregate demand would have to be boosted since it was sinking dramatically as the long binge of consumer spending went into reverse and people drew in their horns and attempted to pay off accumulated debts.

The authorities set about their tasks with the relish of someone sucking lemons. In the UK, Prime

Minister Gordon Brown, with ten years standing as Chancellor of the Exchequer before taking on that role, together with the Chancellor, Alistair Darling, had spent the previous decade courting and lauding the City of London and turned a blind eye to its excesses whereby senior bank executives were paying themselves and their traders obscenely high salaries and bonus packages. No wonder the Labour government was reticent about bringing in controls. They must also be held responsible for allowing the unconstrained long boom in house prices and its accompanying consumer spending spree, funded in part by equity releases from soaring property values.

Now they were faced with clearing up the mess that they had been instrumental in creating whilst trying to claim it was all a global phenomenon. The Queen posed the right question to a group of economists on a visit to the London School of Economics in 2008: 'Why did no-one see it coming?' she asked. In fact there were some lone academic wolves baying their warnings in the wilderness but nobody listened.

Brown and Darling, through the Bank of England, addressed the problem of the under-capitalisation of the banks causing the credit squeeze by combining the 'bailout' loans to banks with a policy of 'Quantitative Easing' (QE). The latter meant that the Bank would in effect create electronic money to purchase 'gilts' – i.e. fixed interest securities issued by the government – from the banks in an attempt to get them to on-lend the cash to businesses and individuals. QE would be launched in phased tranches up to a maximum of a mind-blowing £200 billion. This figure was reached early in 2010 and the effect so far has been somewhat underwhelming in that banks have tended to use the money to restore their balance sheets and their capital base while charging high rates of interest relative to the Bank of England's low official rate of 0.5 per cent for any business loans. Hence the air is blue with the squeals of pain from small businesses desperately anxious about their failing attempts to obtain loans to tide them over this deepest of all recessions.

Barack Obama's administration is facing the same problem in the United States. In frustration at their collective sloth, Obama summoned the bosses of nine major banks to a summit in Washington in December 2009 to express his irritation that despite the government's bailout package of $700 billion (£430 billion), small businesses across the country were struggling to obtain loans and credit. He did not mince his words: 'America's banks received extraordinary assistance from American taxpayers to rebuild their industry.' He told the press after the meeting. 'Now that they're back on their feet, we expect an extraordinary commitment from them to help rebuild our economy.'

This is as good a place as any to stop recording the key origins and features of the financial and economic crisis and, in the last chapter, return to one of the questions with which this one opened. What do these events portend for the future?

13

Ideological Epilogue

Only a fool would attempt to forecast the outcome of corrective policies put in place a matter of months before the start of the second decade of the twenty-first century. But it is possible to speculate a little on the two main themes emerging from the scribblings of commentators and academics bold enough to con-tribute their oracular offerings from studying their own particular runes. The first camp of soothsayers looks at the impact of the crisis on economies and offers certain solutions. The second camp looks at the impact on economics and its ideological implications. We shall sample both in this chapter.

John Kay, visiting professor at the LSE writing in *The Guardian* in March 2009, was nothing if not succinct in his analysis and solution. He pinned the cause of the credit crunch on what he called 'casino-utility attachment'. The utility was the payment sys-tem along with the deposits and lending that com-mercial banks undertake which are essential for the functioning of the non-financial economy – in a phrase, mine not Professor Kay's, the 'boring bits of banking'. The casino implies the risky trading activity of investment banking which is akin to gambling. Plainly, the losses of the casino undermined the utility bringing it to a standstill. Hence, to quote Professor Kay, 'The problem points directly to the solution – permanent separation of the utility and the casino'.

Taking a global view as befits the UN commission of experts on reforms of the international monetary and financial system chaired by the Nobel economist, Joseph Stiglitz, its report early in 2009 foresaw the greatest impact falling on LDCs, with the prospect of 30–50 million more people unemployed in 2009 compared with 2007. Without rapid action to counter the impact of the crisis, the report warns that a further 200 million people could be pushed into poverty. It worries about national governments looking after their own citizens first and resorting to protectionist measures harmfully affecting LDCs in particular. Whilst there is a growing consensus about the need for countries to adopt fiscal stimulus policies, LDCs don't have sufficient resources to do so and will need assistance to expand their economies without the usual conditions exhorting them to contract spending and raise interest rates.

Stiglitz also argues for stronger regulation with reforms going beyond the financial sector to tackle the corporate governance which encouraged excessive risk-taking, and the inadequate competition laws which allowed banks to grow so large that they were thought to be too big to fail. The BBC's distinctive commentator throughout the crisis, Robert Peston, made a similar point in a radio broadcast at the start of 2010. He claimed that banking experts, especially those hibernating in Basel, are devising new regulatory reforms supposedly correcting the faults in the existing regulatory regime. But these so-called experts are the very same people whose light-touch regulations led the banking system to the edge of the cliff, causing its near demise. Furthermore, their political masters, to whom they are supposedly answerable, know even less about how the crisis happened. How on earth will improved arrangements emerge from these sources, he asks?

The system is also totally outside democratic control yet it's the populace at large who are going to pick up the enormous bill for this drunken financial binge in the form of higher taxes and public expenditure cuts, damaging national services such as health and education for years to come. No wonder the people of Iceland have forced their government to hold a constitutional referendum on whether their country should repay debts to countries such as the Netherlands and UK whose citizens lost money deposited in Icelandic banks. Why should they be held responsible for the profligacy of their banks? You can see their point.

Learning from these crisis events, Stiglitz sees a need for a totally new international institutional framework consisting of a global regulatory authority, a global competition authority and a global reserve system. Some of us think we've been here before. Wasn't the IMF a kind of bank sorting out equitably the problems facing deficit countries with the bounties from surplus countries? Then again, wasn't the World Bank a kind of fund assisting poor countries with development finance lent at low interest rates or awarded as grants? Where did it all go wrong? At any rate, we might echo the sentiment of Thomas Balogh nearly forty years ago when he concluded his little book[27] on international monetary reform with the prescient words, 'under no circumstances should the bankers again be allowed to wreck the world'.

In the voice of one banking Chief Economist, Gerard Lyons of Standard Chartered, concern was expressed about triggering excessive regulation which would reduce the credit that drives trade and investment. He wants emerging economies led by China to save less and spend more to get the world out of recession. In his view:

> Imbalances in the global economy and a systemic collapse in the financial system caused this crisis. The G20 [i.e. the world's major developed and developing economies which were about to gather in April 2009 for a conference on the crisis] must move us to a future where the world economy is balanced and the financial system fixed.[28]

Nothing too revolutionary being advocated here then – just a simple plea for paradise on earth.

By contrast, a more radical approach is offered by Heiner Flassbeck of UNCTAD, who sides with the Federal Reserve's Chairman, Ben Bernanke's

---

[27] Balogh, T. and Balacs, P. (1973) *Fact and Fancy in International Economic Relations*. Oxford: Pergamon Press, p. 84.
[28] *The Guardian*, 23 March 2009.

aggressive action to restore the flow of credit. He also wants the G20 to:

> ... close down the casino and put financial markets back in the hands of governments. There are people waiting in the City of London to get back to the gambling game. Governments have said, we won't intervene, let the market decide – but they have to realise they are as informed as any other market participants.[29]

This sample of opinions from the first camp of commentators provides the flavour of a spate of articles reflecting on the impact the recession might have on economies, and the policy responses that might get us out of the mess. The recurring solutions can be briefly summarised as some combination of the following:

- Tougher regulation of banks and removal of their 'casino' functions.
- Monetary injections to the financial system to lower interest rates and revive lending to business and consumers.
- Government intervention to boost aggregate demand.
- Protection of vulnerable LDCs.
- Reform of global financial relations.

Strange as it seems, recovery of a sort is in the wind. From the confidence-draining panic towards the end

---

[29] *The Guardian*, 23 March 2009.

of 2008, in a little over a year the plunge into negative figures for international trade and economic growth was halted and partially reversed. Stock markets began to climb again around the world, house prices began rising and banks bounced back into profit. The infamous 'green shoots' of economic recovery were being spotted all over the place. As for the banks, astonishingly, even in those like Northern Rock and the Lloyds Banking Group, rescued and now largely owned by the British government, the talk is once again all about huge profits being made and the need to reward the staff who cleverly made them with commensurately large bonuses. Otherwise they will be poached by rival firms in the intensely competitive international markets for such rare talent.

But hang on a minute. It doesn't take a genius to make a profit when your bank has privileged access to the central bank to borrow funds at less than 1 per cent, lend them out at around 7 per cent and watch the returns roll in. QE has unleashed huge amounts of cash into the financial system so is it any wonder that a lot of it finds its way from investors into riskier equity markets, driving up their prices and offering the prospect of higher dividends than the meagre interest rates earned on deposit accounts? On the face of it, it looks like *déjà vu* all over again and that spells danger. Not for nothing did *The Economist* for 9–15 January 2010 sport a cover title saying, 'Bubble Warning – why assets are overvalued'.

Turning to the second camp of observers witnessing the unravelling of the mainstream economic model operating over the last thirty years, leaving the reputation of economics and its practitioners equally sullied in its wake, we find leading exponents of the 'dismal science' warring among themselves. The ideological debate was summarised in an article in *The Economist* [18 July 2009] entitled 'The other-worldly philosophers' and, in this final section of the chapter, I make no apology for drawing on some of its arguments and quotations to illustrate the turmoil which appears to be affecting the discipline of economics.

Essentially it seems like a re-run of the conflict between monetarists and Keynesians which was raging in the 1970s but with more aggro. Macro-economics was invented by John Maynard Keynes and articulated in his seminal work, *The General Theory of Employment, Interest and Money* in 1936. It was controversial because it challenged the conventional wisdom of classical economic theory that held that supply creates its own demand and that prices in competitive markets for goods and services and for the factors of production land, labour and capital would adjust so that the natural state of an economy would move towards equilibrium. This would be achieved by a freely operating price mechanism, without interference from government, clearing markets and absorbing all resources at the level of full employment.

The facts of the situation in the 1930s Depression with massive unemployment belied this theoretical analysis. It did not matter how low interest rates fell as the price for borrowing money, business confidence was so negative that entrepreneurs remained unwilling to take out loans for investment. It may not be rational but Keynes took the view that 'The markets are moved by animal spirits, and not by reason'.

191

Trying to use interest rates in this way has been described as trying to push on a string. It can't be done. As Keynes once said to a critic, 'When the facts change, I change my mind. What do you do, sir?' Keynes changed his mind, left the mainstream accepted theory of the day and there's been trouble ever since. Diehard establishment classical economists stood their ground, arguing along with Professor Pigou that the reason for high unemployment was not because their theoretical model was wrong but because workers refused to accept lower wages. The market was prevented from working properly due to institutional frictions such as trade unions interfering with it. The argument about the stickiness of wage rates in a downward direction fed the ideological debate for many years.

In the meantime Keynesian ideas took root, especially the idea that public investment should plug the gap when private investment is insufficient to get the economy out of the doldrums. Government expenditure on re-armament proved empirically Keynes's theory of employment and after the Second World War Keynesians ruled the roost for the next thirty years. Their ideas became the new orthodoxy and full employment via demand management the key aim of economic policy whichever political party formed the government.

Eventually, the ideological pendulum swung back again towards the old conservative model but in a new guise. The Keynesian approach came under attack from the gnomic arch monetarist, Professor Milton Friedman, who hosted a 'Money and Banking' workshop at the University of Chicago and was leader of the 'Chicago School' of economics and a vigorous opponent of active intervention by the government whether to correct instability in the economy or in any other sphere of human behaviour. As a libertarian he believed that governments only made matters worse and individuals should be left alone in the conduct of their affairs, including their economic activities. His ideas were given greater prominence when western governments were having difficulty using fiscal and monetary policy to deal with the high inflation of the 1970s associated with the dramatic increases in oil prices in 1973 and 1979/80 by OPEC. As a result, almost single-handedly, Friedman had restored money to the frontline of economic analysis, arguing that inflation was entirely a monetary phenomenon and a rate of growth should be fixed for the supply of money compatible with steady or zero inflation in the long run.

Price inflation increased if an economy was growing fast and meeting capacity limits on production when operating towards the full employment level of output. Hence, constraining the supply of money to squeeze inflation out of the system slowed the growth rate and increased the level of unemployment. Nevertheless, Friedman's harsh policy remedy was warmly welcomed by the Thatcher government led by its Chancellor of the Exchequer, Geoffrey Howe, as it drove the level of unemployment up to 3 million in the early 1980s under the slogan 'no gain without pain'. Despite this evidence of its damaging impact, Friedmanite monetarist philosophy pervaded the groves of academic economics and stalked the corridors of power for many years until its sudden demise with the recent collapse in its superficially more sophisticated expressions in the current banking crisis.

Outspoken critics of this philosophy within the American economics profession include Brad DeLong of the University of California, Berkeley, and Paul Krugman of Princeton. In his Lionel Robbins lecture at the LSE in June 2009, Krugman claimed that most macroeconomics of the past thirty years was 'spectacularly useless at best, and positively harmful at worst'. DeLong accused Nobel prizewinner, Robert Lucas, of the University of Chicago, of 'making ancient and basic analytical errors all over the place' and Harvard's Robert Barro of 'making truly boneheaded arguments'. Both are towering figures in the discipline of macroeconomics.

The defenders of high-tech developments in economics, clutching their mathematical models, deny that their methods are responsible for the credit crunch and accuse their critics of 'falling back on antiquated Keynesian doctrines – as if nothing had been learned in the past 70 years'. Likewise, the 'critics accuse economists like Mr Lucas of *not* falling back on Keynesian economics – as if everything had been forgotten over the past 70 years'. With statements like these the malaise among economists is clearly deepening and things are getting ugly. Writs will be flying if this goes on much longer.

Meanwhile, here in the UK we do things rather differently. Cloaked in moderation and politeness, twenty economists wrote a letter to *The Sunday Times* (14 February 2010) more or less siding with the opposition Conservative Party in its criticism of the

Labour government for not beginning to cut the enormous government debt incurred in preventing a collapse of the banking system without delay. This would help to pacify overseas investors who were getting twitchy over the size of the UK's debt, raising doubts over its ability to repay their loans as holders of UK government securities. Less than a week later, on 19 February, sixty economists in two equally measured and courteous letters to the *Financial Times* backed the government's stance in *not* applying the brakes too soon for fear of snuffing out the fragile signs of recovery in the economy and before sustainable economic growth had been restored.

Hence this chapter ends with the argument and the economy nicely poised on the edge of this policy precipice shortly to be resolved after the forthcoming General Election expected in early May 2010. Or perhaps not, if neither of the main political parties gains an overall majority in the House of Commons and there's a hung parliament. What exciting times we live in!

We shall discreetly take our leave while both sides of the ideological divide are fighting like ferrets in a sack. One-handed economists advocating theories and policies which reflect their own political standpoints are back on centre stage. Perhaps they never really left it.

Afterword

After the general election on 6 May 2010, the UK entered uncharted territory. Not having won an overall majority, the Conservative Party, headed by David Cameron, successfully negotiated a deal with the Liberal Democrats, headed by Nick Clegg, to form a coalition government with the two leaders becoming Prime Minister and Deputy Prime Minister respectively. With five Cabinet posts and around a total of twenty posts in government held by the Lib Dems, the operational integration of the two governing parties made it almost feel like a merger.

Politically, everything changed, but economically the key fault lines remained the same as in the general conclusion of the last chapter, except that the ideological policy gap had widened and the dichotomy of views regarding policy appeared superficially to have become more deeply entrenched. The argument was still about timing. Both sides recognised the need for the UK and other European countries to reduce their historically high government debts, but centre-left leaning commentators felt there would be problems if this was done too quickly and centre-right commentators thought it much more dangerous to delay implementing the necessary tough remedies.

This divergence was nicely brought out in an article[30] analysing movements on the UK stock exchange where share prices had been bouncing around like corks in a hurricane in the summer of 2010. The headline read, 'Bull vs Bear: who's right about FTSE's[31] recovery?'. In the article, two financial gurus considered the same phenomena, epitomised by a 6.1 per cent surge in the 'footsie' index, and reached diametrically opposed conclusions about the state of the economy and therefore the prospects for financial investments in equities.

The Bull saw a rosy future for shares, believing that we had weathered the economic storm and that globally economic growth would be sustained, boosted by expansion in emerging markets in countries such as Argentina and India. With the recovery, sales were rising, increasing companies' profits. Long-term interest rates were low, reflecting the fact that overseas investors were willing to purchase UK government securities (which is the way we fund our debts). This suggested that they had confidence in the way the British government was tackling its problems. In short, the Bull's advice was that this was a good time to buy shares in companies with a global reach.

The Bear, by contrast, was very gloomy and painted a much darker picture. He pointed to five previous 'easy credit' booms created by governments when stock markets rose and interest rates were low, leading to massive private sector debt. The policy medicine each time was to move to cut public sector

[30] *The Daily Telegraph*, 10 July 2010.
[31] FTSE: *Financial Times* Stock Exchange 100 Share Index.

expenditure, in the expectation that the debt-ridden private sector would expand and plug the gap. But why should it, given that people would be reluctant to borrow if they were fearful about losing their jobs? The same applied to firms facing falling sales. Banks would also be unwilling to lend to either. When the public expenditure cuts took effect and unemployment increased, the downward spiral would be *strengthened* as a result of reduced incomes leading in turn to falls in people's expenditure on consumption. Hence, for the Bear, this was the time to sell shares!

As it happens, it won't be long before there is empirical evidence in support of the general thrust of one of these views, and not limited to the prospect for shares. The coalition government has begun taking steps to reduce the approximate £170 billion deficit inherited from the Labour government and the name of the game is austerity. Governments have two choices when they're spending more than their income, and borrowing the difference becomes excessive in the eyes of their creditors. They can either put up taxes to increase revenue or cut government expenditure. It's usually a bit of both. The Labour government was planning to halve the deficit over four years, roughly in the proportions 60 per cent from expenditure cuts and 40 per cent from tax increases. The coalition's Chancellor of the Exchequer, George Osborne, in an emergency budget, set out to remove the *whole* deficit over the life of the Parliament (i.e. five years), with government expenditure cuts bearing the brunt of nearly 80 per cent of the total and tax increases contributing just over 20 per cent.

The division between the opposition Labour Party and the Conservative/Lib Dem coalition is stark. The latter is in a hurry to restore fiscal balance and much more draconian in its approach. Critics argue that the emphasis on expenditure cuts bears down hardest on those who have no choice but to use public services. It is therefore regressive, as is the increase in VAT announced in the budget, because it cannot be avoided on essential purchases and hurts lower-income groups most. Direct taxation can be more progressive by charging higher rates on the wealthy and lower or zero rates on the poor.

If the government achieves its aim (and it's a big 'if' since governments have notoriously failed to cut back expenditure in the past despite their intentions), then with the NHS and international aid ring-fenced against cuts, other individual government departments will have to cut expenditure by 25 per cent or more. The implications for unemployment are difficult to contemplate, but a great many public sector employees may lose their jobs in the fairly near future unless widespread social unrest – as occurred in Greece in 2010 – forces the government to retreat.

The other big imponderable is how quickly the private sector will move with entrepreneurial zeal in response to government policy carrots to invest in business and create new jobs, taking up the slack left by the diminished public sector. As *The Economist* put it, in an article[32] headed 'Osborne's gamble', 'He [George Osborne] calls it [the budget] business-friendly, and so it is widely regarded. But it is also a

---

[32] *The Economist*, 26 June–2 July 2010.

gamble: that the private sector will become an engine of growth as public sector spending falls.' If now is the time to place bets, as an incorrigible optimist, I should side with the Bull's analysis but I fancy the odds favour the darker scenario proposed by the Bear. At least we can say we are witnessing a rare experiment in economic policy. An unprecedentedly high government deficit is being treated with the biggest retrenchment in our history and no one really knows what will happen. The economy will either bounce back into steady growth after a few very lean, austere years, or sink into a 1930s' slump.

Are we staring into the abyss of a possible 'double dip recession'? Yes we are. Certainly *The Guardian* correspondent, Simon Jenkins,[33] thinks so. Economic growth is negligible, the banks have largely absorbed the huge dollops of money from QE to shore up their balance sheets and shed toxic assets instead of lending to small businesses. Net lending to business is still negative. In other words, in the middle of 2010, after more than a year of QE, businesses were repaying loans faster than new loans were being created. At the same time, pay freezes were being introduced, redundancies were about to increase and only the maintenance of public expenditure was keeping the economy afloat. When the proposed cuts in expenditure begin to hit home, if the government sticks to its policy of pushing up VAT early in 2011, private consumption spending will fall through the floor. For Simon Jenkins this is to 'ignore Keynes's simple insight that businessmen will not invest and the

---

[33] *The Guardian*, 14 July 2010.

economy will not grow if there is no consumer demand for products'. We'd better fasten our safety belts as we could be heading for a roller-coaster ride on the Big Double Dipper.

Where does all this leave economics? As the economic crisis unfolded, an unbridled adherence to a market philosophy was seen to be the culprit by building a culture of excessive rewards into financial systems through the over-creation of dubious derivatives resting on the basis of candy floss. The scourge spread like wildfire across the globe and, as the emptiness at its base was revealed, it unravelled with equal speed, threatening the world economy with collapse.

Against that background, there was much talk of a new paradigmatic approach to economics as a subject incorporating dynamic rather than static models, allowing for evolution of economic systems premised on processes of disequilibrium rather than equilibrium and letting history, development and political economy reassert themselves in discourse and research. Certainly the ahistorical, narrow, distorted orthodoxy of neoclassical economics which some think led us into this mess was being challenged. It was hoped that it would be replaced in the groves of academe and economic policy-making by something finer, more rounded and ethically sound. Sadly, that does not appear to be happening. Instead, despite mainstream economists' belief in a fundamentally flawed theory of how a market economy operates, as evidenced by the 2008 crash in asset markets beneath a mountain of debt, it will still be the case according to Steve Keen, that 'The battle against neoclassical economic orthodoxy within universities will be long and hard, even though its failure will be apparent to those in the non-academic world'.[34] If he's right, it will be some time before the bulk of the economics profession gets its hands dirty again in the real world.

---

[34] Keen, S. (2009) 'Mad, bad and dangerous to know', *Real-world Economics Review*, no. 49, pp. 1–7, see http://www.paecon.net/PAEReview/issue49/keen49.pdf.

Further Reading

If your romp through this little tome has whetted your appetite for more, as a fully-fledged one-handed economist I can freely advocate the following selective references.

Uganda

Karugire, S.R. (1988) *The Roots of Instability in Uganda*. Kampala: The New Vision Printing and Publishing Corporation.

Samwiri Karugire was a colleague and friend in the 1960s. This little book, though poorly printed, is full of an insider's insights as it traces the chequered history of Uganda from the background to independence in 1962 to the assumption of power by President Yoweri Museveni in 1986.

Museveni, Y.K. (1997) *Sowing the Mustard Seed*. London: Macmillan.

This is the autobiography of Yoweri Museveni from his childhood among the Banyankore Bahima cattle-keepers in south-eastern Uganda to leader of a guerrilla army of liberation from the tyranny of Idi Amin and his successors, and ultimately to become President in 1986.

Bangladesh

Chen, M.A. (1986) *A Quiet Revolution: Women in Transition in Rural Bangladesh*. Dhaka: BRAC Prokashana.

The Bangladesh Rural Advancement Committee (BRAC) is a private, non-governmental development institution founded and managed by Bangladeshis. This book describes and assesses BRAC's efforts to help poor rural women with projects designed to improve their lives. It presents BRAC's methodology of development and depicts in detail examples of how it is being implemented.

Hartman, B. and Boyce, J.K. (1988) *A Quiet Violence: View from a Bangladesh Village*. Dhaka: Dhaka University Press.

Betsy Hartman and James Boyce were expatriate Americans who decided to study and learn about rural life in Bangladesh by staying in one village for nine months. This is a fascinating account of their experience.

Aspects of development

Bryant, C. and White, L.G. (1984) *Managing Rural Development with Small Farmer Participation*. West Hartford, CT: Kumarian Press.

This is a little gem of a book. A short, practical manual for those engaging with poor farmers endeavouring to improve their incomes. It employs the 'prisoners' dilemma' argument to good effect in overcoming the 'free rider' problem which inhibits participation in collective action.

Clark, J. (1991) *Democratizing Development*. London: Earthscan Publications.

John Clark knows voluntary development organisations as an insider who worked for many years at one of the oldest NGOs, OXFAM, before taking his expertise to the World Bank and later the UN Secretary-General's Office. He declares the message of his book in these words: 'Voluntary organisations will only achieve their full potential if they develop a more strategic, co-ordinated way of working. Their projects are important and will remain so, but in themselves do no more than create islands of relative prosperity within an increasingly hostile sea.' Twenty years on, my guess is that the message still applies.

Cooke, B. and Kothari, U. (eds.) (1981) *Participation: The New Tyranny?* London: Zed Books.

A serious collection of essays and case studies offering a timely criticism of the way in which the language of discourse on development has obscured the way in which 'participation' actually means behaving in conformity with the objectives set by others.

de Rivero, O. (2001) *The Myth of Development: The Non-Viable Economies of the 21st Century*. London: Zed Books.

A sobering account of how little has been achieved after more than fifty years of international initiatives to develop poor countries. Oswaldo de Rivero, from his vantage point as a Peruvian diplomat who represented his country at succesive rounds of negotiations under the General Agreement on Tariffs and Trade (GATT) and other world forums, concludes that many LDCs are not on the road to becoming newly industrialised countries like South Korea or Taiwan. Rather, they are slipping towards the status of becoming nonviable national economies.

Schultz, T. W. (1964) *Transforming Traditional Agriculture*. New Haven, CT: Yale University Press.

A classic of its day, showing that, far from being lazy peasants, farmers in traditional agriculture were efficient economic operators given the state of technical knowledge at their disposal.

Project analysis

Price Gittinger, J. (1982) *Economic Analysis of Agricultural Projects,* 2nd edn. Baltimore, MD: The Johns Hopkins University Press.

Having relied heavily on this comprehensive text in my teaching and practice as a development economist, it was a privilege to meet Price Gittinger when he came out to Swaziland in 1986 as head of a World Bank mission to advise CDC on the future development of their Mananga Agricultural Management Centre during my tenure as Principal. His authoritative book covers all aspects of project appraisal, has proved to be one of the World Bank's most popular titles and is used extensively in universities and in the field.

Hirschman, A.O. (1967) *Development Projects Observed*. Washington: The Brookings Institution.

Albert Hirschman was one of the giants in the study of economic development and a bit of a maverick. Here he looks at eleven different development projects in an effort to discover how agencies and other organisations actually carry out development. He finds that each project is 'a unique constellation of experiences and consequences'. Hence it is impossible to make generalisations about what makes for success and failure in implementing projects. In a wonderful turn of phrase he concludes modestly that he has, 'pursued in these pages what could only be a mirage – the snatching of systematic insight from casual hindsight'. In fact, there is nothing casual at all in what he gleans from this year-long backward look at projects that have already been completed.

Critiques of economics

Akerlof, G. A. and Shiller, R. J. (2009) *Animal Spirits: How Human Psychology Drives the Economy, and Why it Matters for Global Capitalism*. Princeton, NJ: Princeton University Press.

The authors reinstate the Keynesian idea of 'animal spirits' as the driving force behind the financial crises in the latter years of the first decade of the twenty-first century. In their view, managing them in the subsequent recession needs the steady hand of government on the tiller. Markets alone can't do it.

Galbraith, J. K. (1958) *The Affluent Society*. London: Hamish Hamilton.

John Kenneth Galbraith was one of the few economists who deliberately wrote for a wider audience. His books are works of literature and usually challenge conventional wisdom in economics. Early on in this pathbreaking book, Galbraith makes it clear that he thinks 'very little of certain of the central ideas of economics'. In it he spotlights the imbalance between performance in the private sector of the American economy which creates artificial needs for new goods of marginal significance and persuades people to buy them, with that of the public sector which somehow neglects to provide enough essential services such as parks, playgrounds and police.

Galbraith, J. K. (1975) *Money: Whence it Came, Where it Went*. London: André Deutsch.

This is a good, solid history of money but includes his trademark challenge to accepted ideas by questioning the conventional uses of monetary and fiscal policies.

Johnson, S. (2009) 'The quiet coup', http://www.theatlantic.com/doc/200905/imf-advice.

Simon Johnson, a former chief economist of the IMF, draws parallels between his work with teams from the IMF assisting client countries seeking a loan when they've been living beyond their means, and the situation facing the USA and other developed countries that have also gone on a spending spree that they could not afford. For dealing with that and the subsequent financial crisis, the medicine of expenditure cutbacks and curtailing overborrowing and excessive credit is similar in each case. This article presents a troubling tale of the incestuous relationship between Wall Street and Washington, with powerful bankers being involved with government officials that have frequently worked in the same financial institutions. Both groups work together when sorting out the mess they have also been involved in creating.

Seers, D. and Joy, L. (eds) (1971) *Development in a Divided World*. Harmondsworth: Penguin.

All aspects of development economics are critically assessed in this book written by Fellows of the Institute of Development Studies at the University of Sussex which was established as an independent centre for research, teaching and consultancy by the then Ministry of Overseas Development.

Taibbi, M. (2009) 'The big takeover', *Rolling Stone*, 1075, 2 April, http://www.rollingstone.com/politics/story/ 26793903/the_big_takeover.

Matt Taibbi covers some of the same ground as Simon Johnson in a brilliant expletive-ridden, blow-by-blow account, from the bailing-out of AIG through the whole sorry saga of the near collapse of the American financial system. His side heading after the title describes his central theme: 'The global economic crisis isn't about money – it's about power. How Wall Street insiders are using the bailout to stage a revolution'. As a piece of invective it's as gripping as a page-turning whodunnit. It's almost as if Taibbi was in the room when crucial meetings were held to stop the crisis. Perhaps he was. At any rate it confirms his status as an investigative journalist.

Ward, B. (1972) *What's Wrong with Economics?* London: Macmillan.

At a time when behavioural economics is becoming more fashionable, it's fascinating to note that Benjamin Ward was suggesting the need for it nearly forty years ago. His book questions the hierarchical dominance in the economics profession of micro-economics, macroeconomics and econometrics and also raises fundamental issues for discussion in terms of in what sense economics can be regarded as a science. Ward offers a thought-provoking read set in the context of Thomas Kuhn's notion of scientific revolution and a wider philosophical debate about verification and values in economics.

Economic development textbooks

For serious students of economics the following texts may be of interest. They are written by acknowledged experts on the problems of development and since they are comprehensive in themselves are listed without further comments.

Dasgupta, A.K. and Pearce, D.W. (1972) *Cost-Benefit Analysis: Theory and Practice*. London: Macmillan.

Hirschman, A.O. (1958) *The Strategy of Economic Development*. New Haven, CT: Yale University Press.

Meier, G. and Rauch, J.E. (2005) *Leading Issues in Economic Development*, 8th edn. Oxford: Oxford University Press.

Meier, G. and Seers, D. (eds) (1984) *Pioneers in Development*. Oxford: Oxford University Press.

Sen, A. (1984) *Resources, Values and Development*. Oxford: Basil Blackwell.